Praying for Peace

Praying for Peace

Compiled by
MICHAEL HARE DUKE
BISHOP OF ST ANDREWS

Fount
*An Imprint of HarperCollins*Publishers*

First published in Great Britain in 1991 by Fount Paperbacks

Fount Paperbacks is an imprint of
HarperCollinsReligious
Part of HarperCollins Publishers
77–85 Fulham Palace Road, London W6 8JB

Desktop design and typesetting by Simon Jenkins Associates
Printed and bound in Great Britain by
Cox & Wyman Ltd, Reading

Contents

Acknowlegements

The Editor and publishers are grateful for kind permission to use the following material. The prayers by Richard Skinner and Peter Maurin taken from *Prayers for Peacemakers* (Kevin Mayhew), "The Enemy" by Akong Rinpoche from *Taming the Tiger* (Ozalendara Publishing).

Introduction

War releases powerful emotions that bring many people
to prayer. Horrified at the events unfolding or the
potential cost for the future, they want to discover a
power for good equal to the destructiveness unleashed.
This leads to questions "Where is God?", "Does right
prevail?", "How can you pray?"

The following collection of prayers, thoughts and
meditations is an attempt to meet these questions. It is
explicitly a religious book. Beginning from a Christian
viewpoint, it includes Muslim, Jewish, Hindu and
Buddhist contributions. As nations become embattled,
their prayers can become self-justificatory. If we can
draw on the spiritual traditions of all humanity,
compassion and mercy which every faith teaches can
help us find common ground for peacemaking.

The sections of the book are self-contained but follow
a logical pattern. It starts with the facts behind the call
to prayer. It goes on to provide comments and analysis
which might evoke prayer. It moves to emotions and
gives space for feelings to be expressed. It uses evocative
images to encourage the reader to pray, and in the
"Icons of Hope" shows where God might be glimpsed. It
ends with a Quarry of Prayer for private use and Tools
for Worship to be used in groups or congregations.

The contributions were assembled within seven days,

making use of the same generation of advanced technology which beams instant news around the world and guides missiles to their targets.

The immediate response, which came from almost everybody asked to contribute, was a sense of relief at finding some way to express intense feelings. What is written here is an invitation to all who read it to explore their own emotions, find how they can express them and then build a network of compassion to comfort those who are directly bearing the pain, the fear, the suffering.

Beyond the present crisis is the wider threat to our whole world. Many contributions link together the energy of prayer with action for justice. They reflect a way of love which in a dark time can light a candle of hope. Most importantly they are a witness to the great longing for humanity to discover a new dynamic of peacemaking. Peace belongs to people and will be sustained by everyone's united goodwill. It requires a willingness to share the limited resources of a world which can no longer afford to make competition between individuals and nations the main thrust of its way of life. If that is to be possible it will require a revolution within ourselves and a surrender of our power to the authority of God; that too is what prayer is about.

+ Michael
Bishop's House
Perth
January 1991

8

PART I

The Call to Prayer

The Day it Happened

Good morning. That greeting may sound hollow today. There doesn't seem much good about the first day of another war, especially for those living in the Gulf, serving in the Forces, or their friends and loved ones – perhaps you are among them – at home.

Sometimes I'm asked about the words "Good Friday". It wouldn't be good if the suffering of the Cross were the whole story. But the tragedy of the Cross was followed by the triumph of Easter. Death gave way to new life. This *good* morning we pray that war will give way to peace – and quickly.

We all want peace. And there have been many efforts to obtain peace without conflict in recent months. But peace must never be separated from justice.

The Bible *does* warn us against an easy peace. Jeremiah complained about those who ignored the demands of justice by saying:

> They dress my people's wound, but skin deep only,
> With their saying, "Peace, Peace"
> When there is no peace. (Jeremiah 6:14)

Often we say we're leaving someone in peace when we

11

mean we are simply ignoring them. We cannot ignore the people of Kuwait.

The longer we leave them suffering at the mercy of a barbaric aggressor, the more difficult it will be to create a just order and a lasting peace there – or elsewhere in the world.

The tragedy of war is its cost in human suffering. As a soldier I've seen too much of that to wish it upon others. And it's true that a Christian has a built-in resistance to the use of force. We are to be peacemakers.

But to do justice sometimes compels us to use force. The harsh reality of history is that the use of force has been caused as much by human virtues – our sense of justice, our belief in the difference between right and wrong, our readiness for self-sacrifice on behalf of others – as it has been by any of our failures or wickedness.

Dietrich Bonhoeffer, the German pastor who was killed by the Nazis in the last week of the Second World War, once said that God is among us in our lives, but not on any side.

That's another instinctive Christian insight which helps maintain our reserves of compassion and mercy as we seek to do justice.

Not even in a just war should we forget that pity is Godlike. Nor should we forget, as we seek to do what is right and good, those words of Jesus, "there is only one who is good, that is God" (Matthew 19:17).

And He does not change, nor will He fail us. That is why we can say with conviction even on this bleak day, *Good* morning.

Lord, make Thy will our will in all things, and so give us peace.

Robert Runcie

12

Remembering as a Soldier

I first came here in 1944 when I was a soldier on my way to Normandy to rejoin the war. Before leaving, we were marched into this Cathedral for a memorable service.

Like any group of soldiers, we were a mixed lot. There was the usual bravado, a good deal of nervous joking, and here and there a cynic trying to puncture brave words. And there were the more thoughtful ones, silently keeping their anxiety to themselves, weighed down by the thought of what might lie ahead.

Later, when military action began, the concentration needed was all-consuming. There wasn't much opportunity for reflection, but that service stayed vividly in my mind. It wasn't that I saw a visitation of angels or a blinding light. Rather, I felt a profound sense of calm and assurance. I know my friends felt the same. We couldn't put it into words, but here we felt we were part of a larger destiny. We drew strength from the words of Bunyan that we sang together:

Who would true valour see
Let him come hither
One here will constant be
Come wind, come weather.

Forty-six years later, and human nature hasn't changed. We are at war again. Our cause is just. We seek to liberate the suffering people in Kuwait. But the cost of war is great. No one who has been a soldier would wish its suffering on others. Once again, as always in times of crisis or tragedy, people turn to prayer. Our motives may be muddled, but our instinct is sound. We know our frailty and we ask God for the help and strength we need.

Fifty years ago the whole nation was involved. There

13

was a spirit of solidarity between those at home and those away fighting. Today there are some who are sceptical, unsure about the necessity of war. Yet human sympathy and understanding are always needed, whatever the doubts. All those involved need our support: those who give orders, those who obey them and those affected by them. They need our concern, our love and understanding.

And, if we can, our prayers. We place our fears and hopes in God's hands. We ask him to strengthen what is good, and bring good out of what is evil. Faith does not consist in believing impossible things. Our faith is that Christ's promises won't fail. He is with us in sorrow, in anxiety, in danger.

At a time like this, all of us have our own personal feelings and private thoughts – for a son or daughter, brother, husband or friend. We need reassurance, the sort that only God can give, as this prayer of St Teresa expresses:

Let nothing disturb thee,
Nothing affright thee;
All things are passing;
God never changeth;
Patient endurance
Attaineth to all things;
Who God possesseth
In nothing is wanting
Alone God sufficeth.

Robert Runcie

The background from which he spoke was his experience as a tank commander in World War II. He recalled that in a TV broadcast on Sunday 20 January from the Crypt of Canterbury Cathedral.

14

A Cardinal's Compassion

A friend of mind called early yesterday morning on his way to work. He told me that shortly after hearing that the conflict in the Gulf had begun he looked at his baby daughter, wondering what kind of world this child had been born into. I understood how he was feeling and surely, of course, we all do. The news that the fighting had started made me feel very depressed. I couldn't get out of my mind the horror and tragedy that war always is. And the news of the bombing of Tel Aviv and Haifa in the early hours of this morning has left me even more anxious. These are going to be dark days indeed.

Then, strangely, and in spite of all, a different thought has been playing in my mind: this war will not be in vain. So many people have agonised over the rights and wrongs of going to war, so many have prayed and held vigils – something good must come out of all that effort, and that prayer cannot go unheard. I began to realize once again that so often in the darkness we can in fact see a glimmer of light; out of despair new hope is born.

The fear of that young father is also the source of his determination and courage. He knows the kind of world he wants for his daughter. He longs for a world in which the dignity of every person is respected, and justice for each assured. He wants her to grow up in a nation whose identity, history and rights are recognized. And he wants, for her, a world in which nations work together, partners in a greater unity, responsive to each other's needs and able, through the United Nations, to sustain order and peace.

I am speaking about a great ideal. It's to look on the world as God sees it; it's to obey His will and to achieve His purpose. We too often frustrate God's design, and we are never free from blame. None the less even in these dark days we must not lose sight of this vision.

Saddam Hussein has indeed sinned against it. He has ignored the resolutions of the United Nations, attempted to wipe a sovereign state off the map, and trampled on the rights of so many in his own country and in Kuwait. It's for the sake of these thousands of people, suffering so grievously; it's for the restoration of a nation; and it's to uphold the authority of the United Nations, that war is now upon us.

Like that young man I wish that there could have been another way. But it's not so. Yet so many prayers and so much sacrifice will not be in vain if, after the conflict, a new and better order emerges. Only when truth and justice are respected can there be a true peace. And only with God's help will this be achieved.

Then that little girl can grow up in a happier and safer world. That must be our earnest prayer today.

Basil Hume

A Pastoral Letter

Dear Sisters and Brothers,

What we have feared has come to pass. What lies ahead only God knows. We hold in our hearts all who are caught in the agony of battle. Particularly we pray for the brave men and women of the military forces, for those who wait at home, and for all the innocent caught in the horror of the battle.

The future is unclear but our response is certain, and we turn to God in prayer.

Let us pray:

that the conflict may come to a speedy and decisive end, and

16

that those at risk be safely delivered

that the relationships of the nations be healed

that weapons of mass destruction not be used

that our spirits may not be inflamed by hatred

that international humanitarian law (the "Geneva Conventions") be strictly applied and adhered to

that refugees find safe haven in countries removed from the conflict

that we may be granted the spirit of repentance and reconciliation

that our President, George, be upheld by our prayers, and that he and all the leaders of the nations may be guided in their decisions by the Spirit of mercy and peace.

I must emphasize that many thousands of faithful people in this country and abroad have prayed and marched for a peaceful resolution of the Gulf crisis. Some, myself included, have long believed that war was uncalled for, that options short of war were far from being exhausted. It is now left for us to continue to pray and work for peace. I am heartened that people around our church are doing just that. Even in the heat of battle let us not forget that the call to peacemaking is an imperative for Christians.

I will continue my peacemaking efforts in co-operation with other religious leaders. Strategies for peacemaking will develop as events unfold and I will share them with you. Such efforts must continue in strength, and be guided by repentance rather than righteousness.

My dear friends, in closing I want to tell you that I know we are fearful. Let us acknowledge our fears before God and ask that we may feel the sheltering arms of Jesus Christ. Our fear, our anguish, our grief is part of our humanity. We could not be alive to our world's realities and be untouched. As we follow in the path of Christ, we mould ours into compassionate hearts and we open our selves, as He did, to the wounds that come from loving. Let us make ourselves vulnerable in this way, knowing that Christ will take our pain and transform us.

May the peace of God which passes all understanding be with all of His global family.

Edmond Browning

A Voice from Japan

Amid the present hardships of humankind, we, the people of faiths, will never lose hope. We are intent not to give up our efforts to explore the ways of restoring peace as soon as possible in international community. We do firmly believe that we are enjoined by our faith and conscience to love and respect life and to engage in activities in the service of peace and justice.

Our prayers have to be followed by our concrete actions. In co-operation with other world religious organizations, we will take various steps as are deemed necessary, such as addressing joint statements to the parties of the conflict, the Security Council and the member states of the UN, and other relevant bodies; to render aid and service to war victims and refugees; to hold peace prayer meetings, peace demonstrations,

18

peace marches, peace offerings and so on.

May grace and guidance from on high be with all and every one of us, so that we may serve as willing instruments of peace.

Nikkyo Niwano

Germany's Perception

Since the Gulf War began we have started every lecture at the Theology Faculty in Tübingen with a minute's silence, thinking about the war's victims and those responsible, and praying for peace.

On 17 January I presented the following propositions to provide a concluding discussion:

1. This war is not the continuation of politics "by other means" (Clausewitz), but the collapse of any rational kind of politics. With the deadline set for 15 January 1991, not only Saddam Hussein but also the Western politicians gave up their freedom of action and put themselves in a hopelessly tight corner.

2. This war is the consequence of an apocalyptic policy of confrontation. It has been proclaimed by Saddam Hussein as the apocalyptic "mother of all battles" and the final combat of the "believers against the unbelievers". On the Western side, notions of Crusade and apocalyptic images of punishment appear to play a part: Saddam Hussein turns into the "power of evil"; the "civilized world" must bring this barbarian to reason. We have fallen into an apocalyptic suicide trap.

3. According to the doctrine of the "just war", there are

five points in favour of the United Nations' military action, but also two against it:

a) We cannot expect that the situation after the war will be better than the situation before it.
b) The distinction between military and civilian populations can hardly be maintained.

Finally, a war which can lead to the deployment of atomic, biological or chemical weapons can never be a "just war".

4. The West does not understand the Arab mind-set. The Arab world does not understand the West. Demanding an "unconditional" withdrawal from Kuwait leaves Saddam Hussein no way out and has not been geared to the Arab way of thinking.

5. The slogan "No blood for oil" doesn't get it right. At the heart of the conflict lies not oil, but Israel. The cause of this war is the failure of efforts to set up a conference on the Middle East, a conference which would bring peace to the area, and at one and the same time ensure Israel's right to exist and guarantee the Palestinians' right to self-determination. This war will not bring the peoples of the Middle East a single step nearer such a conference, but on the contrary will generate so much bitterness that peace will recede even further into the distance. War is never the way to peace; peace alone is the way to peace.

6. The Middle East was re-shaped in order to create the State of Israel, and the Holocaust shares the blame for making this necessary; for this reason Germany bears a special responsibility for helping the Middle East towards peace. It has taken fifteen years for the Conference of Security and Co-operation in Europe to

20

dismantle the confrontation of the "cold war" and to build up democratic co-operation. We must be patient with the peoples of the Middle East.

Jürgen Moltmann

Message from Jordan

It is neither insignificant nor accidental that religious people from different faiths and denominations have been in the forefront in trying to avert the "shooting war" unleashed last Thursday.

War is unjust by definition. Modern war, given its indiscriminatory nature and the disproportionate suffering it causes to innocents, is even more so. Even before the "shooting war" started, millions of people from the down-trodden of the earth – mainly Asian workers and their dependants – have been the victims of dislocation and suffering. Now the civilians in Iraq are subjected to horror, carnage and death. No better an investment in hatred and continued violence could have been made.

The land of Iraq is overcrowded with cities and sites that have contributed so much to the civilization of man, from Ur of the Chaldeans to Baghdad of the Abbassids, the irreparable destruction of such sites (the historic church of Mar-Thoma [St Thomas] in Nineveh was reportedly hit by aerial bombardment) is a sad comment on modern man's repayment of the debt we all owe to Mesopotamia.

This war will shortly move into a new phase of carnage. This time the victim will be the ecology and the environment, and here, damage can neither be reversed nor wiped out by financial compensation.

These trying times test the moral fibre of believers

the world over. Arms superiority is not moral superiority. Most Muslims take comfort in the fact that men of religion from other faiths have generally approached this tragic conflict with humanism, compassion and wisdom.

We cannot be convinced by arguments that this war is a "tragic necessity". On the contrary, this war could have been avoided – without loss to principle – had quiet and patient diplomacy been given a chance or sanctions more time.

We have never condoned the occupation and annexation of Kuwait, but the destruction of Iraq cannot be but a disproportionally heavy price in human life for an initial wrong. Should evil be corrected by greater evil?

It is ironic and tragic that through a violent act – the Iraqi missile attacks on Tel Aviv and a probable Israeli response, direct or indirect – linkage between the Gulf Crisis and the Arab-Israeli conflict was irrefutably demonstrated. Had the Palestine Question, which stands on its own merit, been addressed before 2 August 1990, no justification could have been found for the attack on Israel.

At these ominous times, men and women of goodwill are called upon to discard the antiquated notion of a "just war". It is easy to apportion blame on this or that leader. However, if we do not all work for an immediate end to this destructive and very dangerous conflict, we shall all have to share in the blame.

El Hassan Bin Talal

What War Means Today

War means – a profligate wastage of money and materials, and, most of all, human lives. Men and women slain or maimed physically and psychologically for life.

War means – a depth of suffering and loss of loved ones borne by parents and children, husbands and wives, which no solace is deep enough to assuage.

War means – an escalation of interracial antagonism which deepens prejudice and leaves a festering hatred which even peace cannot dispel.

War means – ecological disaster affecting this beautiful world of God's creation, our human environment.

War means – that Jesus Christ suffers again the agony of a broken world.

No Christian, or any human being for that matter, would want war. Even a "just war" – which no longer seems possible in this age of nuclear weapons and the means of mass destruction. So what can we do?

We can pray. Pray. Pray.

General Eva Burrows

2

How Shall we Pray?

Jewish Insight

How, then, shall we pray for peace? We have heard from our relatives and friends in Israel, sitting in sealed rooms with their gas masks, waiting for the missiles sent out against them by a warlord who seems almost as Hitler re-born.

We have seen the destruction unleashed by a war where death comes to civilians, to women and children who knew nothing about oil and power politics. We have seen planes fall from the sky, and we know of the young soldiers, on both sides of an almost invisible line, who have died and who will die because the structure of law and justice has been torn apart in our time, because the path of reconciliation and reasoned argument has been forsaken by those who prefer the tools of violence and war.

This much we know: we cannot pray for peace and for Divine protection if we do not extend our concern and compassion to all who suffer at this time. When the world becomes a battle field, everyone suffers. Every war is evil, and a war of self defence – permitted in Jewish and Christian tradition – can only be seen as a necessary, lesser evil which must give way to the process of reconciliation and the striving towards peace at the earliest moment possible. And how can such reconciliation take place if we do not mourn ALL who have died in these dark days? The machinery of war is awesome in our time; the tools for peace are few and fragile. Formal organizations – the United Nations – falter in that task. Yet here in our synagogue, and in many churches, temples, and mosques, prayers for peace rise towards God.

They unite at that point, and cease to be specific pleadings. God's compassion is not limited; it goes out to all humans created to fill the earth. Religions should not, and do not, fight for supremacy with one another on that level. The German philosopher Hermann Cohen once wrote:

> In the face of the community of the spirit, the special characteristics of a specific religion are not to be regarded as limiting factors eliminating the possibility of other religions. The supreme idea of a single reason opens up the possibility of gathering many religions under its wings.

A time of war is not propitious for a call to dialogue among the religions of the world. Nevertheless, it is the right time to remind religions that they must stay aloof from war hysteria; they must not let themselves be used to create hatred against the enemy: "hate sin, not sinners" is a biblical teaching. Throughout the decades of this century of brutality, we have experienced the utmost in suffering; acts of evil have been visited upon the Jewish people in an unparalleled fashion. It has made us more sensitive to the suffering of others, and has directed us to fight evil in every area of life. May our prayers help us to come closer to God in these dark days, and to draw nearer to our neighbour as well. War will be followed by peace, to the time of binding up

26

wounds, to give comfort to all who have suffered. May it also be the time of building bridges among the nations and the religions of the world, so that kindness and compassion will re-emerge upon that "darkling plain where ignorant armies clash by night". We pray for God's protection. We pray for peace.

Albert H Friedlander

What is Happening when we Pray for Others?

Sometimes we have difficulties over prayer for others, simply because we do not stop to think what is happening when we pray. Try to picture the situation.

God is always with us, very close in His love and goodness. At every moment God is here, God is now. When we pray, we do not have to reach out over millions of miles to make contact with God. We simply turn to Him, attend to Him, remember His presence.

The first thing we forget is so obvious. God is just as close all the time to those for whom we pray. We and they are both in His unbounded and unchanging heart. So in prayer we move into a three-cornered relationship – God, them and us; and we all are as near to each other spiritually as it is possible to be.

What happens next? What do we contribute by praying? I believe that the love we have for the person we are praying for is a real channel between us and them, and that God can use that channel to help them. Because we are so close to each other in God's heart, God's own guidance and strength is beamed along the human link set up. By means of our love God can help them make right decisions, have courage and peace deep inside, work better with others, and be supported and strengthened in many other ways.

So things do happen when we pray, which would not happen if we did not. We put our love at God's disposal, and He uses it to do His part. But it is LOVE which makes the link, because only love is in tune with God's own heart.

Those we naturally remember most in prayer – our family and friends – depend for their lives and well-being on many other people. Those people too have their needs, and God loves and cares about them as well. Once we really think what is happening in prayer, our prayers are drawn out in widening circles. We begin to realize that in God's heart we are close to a lot of others who need our prayers.

In war this includes the enemy. It might not be hard to pray, say, for Iraqi troops forced to fight against their will, and for their families. But what about their leaders? If love is the link, can we pray for Saddam Hussein? And yet what could be more important for everyone?

I think we can do it, if we remember that love is basically wanting for the other person what is best for them, not just what would suit us. If we can be with God, caring that what should happen is what is eternally and most deeply best for our enemy's immortal soul, then our prayer can be a link by which God's love can work on them too for the good of all.

Lastly, suppose that what we most want for our own dearest cannot be, because of the world's evil and folly. Even then our love for them in prayer still means that Christ, who is God and who suffered and died on the Cross and rose again, will be helped to bring them through pain and through death itself, and one day reunite us with them in eternal joy.

John Austin Baker

Prayer Beyond Words

"In the same way, the Spirit helps us in our weakness. We do not know what we ought to pray, but the Spirit Himself intercedes for us with groans that words cannot express." These words of Paul in his letter to the Romans (chapter 8, verse 26) echo my plight, mirror my feelings and encourage both my prayer and my faith.

As the inevitability of War in the Gulf became clearer and clearer, and then when we woke up to the reality of its happening, both my heart and my mind felt increasingly numbed. I knew I ought to pray for peace but I could find no clear content for the prayer.

Should it be a pacifist prayer – "Lord, in your Son Jesus, You are wholly against war. Help me to stand out against it and move the people and the leaders of the United Nations and the West to refuse to fight and to find other ways"?

Should it be the reluctant prayer of one convinced that the War although tragic, and perhaps at some earlier stage avoidable, is now the lesser of two evils and so in some way "just"? "Lord I know we ought to have been able to avoid this. Have mercy on us and now that we are engaged in war grant such a sufficient and speedy victory to the UN forces that the killing may stop and we may build a new peace."

Should it be the angry prayer of one who knows that all power is sinfully exploited and that morality is claimed as an ally only when self-interest is sufficiently involved? "Lord, judge our Western arrogance, which uses technological, economic and military superiority to impose our wills on the Arabs and control the oil. Help us to repent for justice and the poor. Let the military might be checked and let the Arabs be free to work together to make their own terms with Israel and us, so that all may live in self-determination and mutual peace."

It is not good enough, is it? I think the confession to God at the beginning of each of my imaginary types of prayer is correct but the request which follows is much more dubious. For it seems that the pacifists do not face the problems of not confronting aggressive power and tyranny; the "just war" supporters do not face up to the evident fact that war is incredibly bloody and solves nothing. The "angries" do not take account of bad motives and power-hungering *on both sides* as endemic in politics between nations, tribes, empires or what you will.

So, I conclude, prayer is not quite like that. Prayer is confession to God of *our* sinfulness, contribution to the mess and present powerlessness. Prayer is a silent and inarticulate reaching out to the love, peace and promise that must be there and can and will somehow be found. Prayer is the readiness to share, in any way we can, in the suffering, the sheer stupidity, the continuing neighbourliness and the resolution to work for peace for all as soon as opportunities come up. Prayer is waiting on God to alert us to the first clue we can see to reassert a concern for common humanity, a common plight and a common need to work together – Arabs, Jews and the rest of us – to build a Middle Eastern settlement out of a shocking amount of suffering, distrust and destruction that should never have happened.

The only *words* I can find are those of the Prayer for Good Friday:

Almighty God, we beseech Thee graciously to behold this Thy family, for which our Lord Jesus Christ was contented to be betrayed and given up into the hands of wicked men, and to suffer death upon the Cross, who now liveth and reigneth with Thee and

30

the Holy Ghost, ever one God, world without end. Amen.

David Jenkins

Lord, Teach us to Pray

When people ask me what I pray for, I smile and say I don't pray *for* anything; I pray because God *is*. I sit before Him open like an empty bowl, like a flower, like a wound. I give Him my joy, my confusion, my boredom, my pain – just lay it there on the floor for Him to process how He wishes and when He is ready. Sometimes He takes my pain away and I am full of a deep and radiant peace, a well of clear and laughing water which spills over into other people's lives. At other times, it is different; it seems that nothing happens. I know nothing but a vast emptiness, the mess of my own life and the chaos of the world. I have learned, however, over many years, that God's silence is like the winter earth in which seeds lie dormant, like the belly of a woman in which a child grows. In His good time, but not before, the darkness will be pierced by light and new life will burst forth.

I think this is one way in which we can pray for peace. When words fail us, when our tears are spent, we can lay them at His feet and wait, in the sure and certain knowledge that even the outcome of this stupid and terrible war is safe in His merciful hands.

Sheila Cassidy

An Oasis on the Battlefield

My stand is naturally that of the Society of Friends, the Quakers, who for 300 years have been pacifists.

The essence of the Quaker attitude to prayer is that one has no right to demand that God should deliver an instant solution to one's problem; instead one must hold the problem up before Him and wait patiently to see what He makes of it. It may be that this joint contemplation will reveal that there is no going back on the inevitable consequences of folly, but that one can nevertheless bring good out of evil in the end.

As the old saying goes, God answers all our prayers – and often the answer is No. In this sense the beginning of prayer is resignation. We have to accept that God is not a Mr Fixit, leaping about the universe correcting our blunders if we ask nicely. There is no escaping the inevitable results of our actions or those of other people, simply by pleading that we didn't mean it and that we'll be good next time. If we have got ourselves into a war then we must take the casualties that come and acknowledge that they are the price of our choice.

But prayer – real prayer that lasts half an hour or more – is an opportunity for calm, for the stilling of passion and frenzy. As a result of prayer we should fight more thoughtfully, mercifully, carefully. If we are going to fight morally it can only be on the grounds that it is the lesser evil, but that involves admitting that an evil it is. If we are going to commit that evil we can only do so in the knowledge of our sinfulness, an awareness that demands prayer.

I have written so far of those who feel they must fight, and I acknowledge that such a conviction can be held sincerely and validly. But as a Quaker I know that I cannot fight, and I regard my pacifism much as a Catholic priest regards his celibacy. It is even a kind of sacrifice.

But I do not hate or despise those who do fight. I get on very well with professional soldiers, and find that we respect each other in a way that does not apply to politicians. I only ask that the fighter prays, too, and thinks out his position as carefully as peace people do.

The Gulf War has been a terrible setback for the peacemaker, and the temptation is to opt out of public life for the duration. But I think that is ignoble. In the renewed prayer for which the situation calls we can be thankful that the pacifist position is at least being given greater respect by governments and media than ever before, and that there is a far greater tenderness towards civilian casualties than was shown in World War II. To an amazing extent the peace movement has made progress and is a force which no civilized government dares now ignore.

Yet peace people must grapple with the fact that Hitler and Stalin and Saddam are genuinely wicked men, and their wickedness cannot be overlooked or forgiven. The faults of democracy do not cancel out the horrors of dictatorship.

I am afraid that however far the peace movement may advance there will always be wickedness and there will always be war. In the end peace is something interior, something personal, something able to survive like an oasis in the desert or a Red Cross tent on the battlefield. We do peace a disservice if we think it stands or falls as a public movement. I suggest that instead of marching and demonstrating we would do better now to concentrate on service to those around us. Service is always the right answer to those wondering "What shall we do?" And that way, by our attitude of calm and prayer, we may hope to infect others with our peacefulness.

Gerald Priestland

Keeping on Praying

At Coventry Cathedral not long ago we were commemorating the fiftieth anniversary of the blanket-bombing of Coventry, and later of German cities like Dresden. The Queen Mother presented the President of Germany with a Cross of Nails, the symbol of reconciliation, and the President gave, from Germany, a Peace Bell. A tablet was unveiled which declares that, "Nation shall not lift up sword against nation, neither shall they learn war any more".

A photographer from The West Midlands Fire Service sent me some photographs of the occasion. In his letter he offered "to take the pictures when Baghdad is given the Cross of Nails in 2041 or, I hope, sooner".

These poignant words summon us all to deepen our prayers for peace. Only Christ's Cross spans the haunting gap between our ideals and intentions and the terrible reality. This means that we must stay close to that Cross.

An Arab friend reminds me that in the Middle East, where the surface is often stony and rocky and harsh and where the bitter divisions of humanity seem to be focused so sharply, underneath have always lain the deepest sources of miracles and of new beginnings. Under the harsh and divided surface of Jerusalem itself runs the buried "Via Dolorosa", the way of Christ's journey to the Cross. All around in the whole area are people, both Jews and Arabs, from the depth of whose being arises continually a profound yearning and capacity for peace and wholeness, scattered, hidden people who can show us what it means to be "the salt of the earth" and "the light of the world".

It is my memory of these people and the invisible bond with them in the Spirit which keeps me praying with them. Underneath Shalom and Salaam, peace, must keep welling up into prayer.

I use the Jesus prayer as a constant rhythm all day.

"Lord Jesus Christ, Son of God, have mercy upon us."

Sometimes I put "have mercy upon me", sometimes, "have mercy on......" and there I put a name or a place, a person or a people. I try to make this prayer the rhythm of my walking, the rhythm of my breathing and living until it becomes a part of me. In this I am drawing on a great tradition which goes back to the deserts of Sinai and Egypt. Let us keep sustaining this rhythm of ceaseless prayer wherever we can, at the same time in our hearts holding before God that area of such sorrow and destruction, and it will still be, as it has ever been, an area of hope, where, deep down, the unbelievable grace of God can still rise to the surface, transfiguring our anxieties, our pain and our sorrow. Let's form a network sustaining each other in this prayer throughout the world.

Simon Barrington-Ward

Prayer in Helplessness

I went to my chapel in the middle of last night after I had heard that war in the Gulf had broken out. I tried to pray. No words came to my lips, no thoughts to my mind. I just felt numb as the horror of what was happening in the Gulf slowly began to sink in. War is always a tragedy however justified it may be. And I feel anguish for so many who tonight know only anxiety and sorrow.

When I tried to pray last night I felt helpless. That sense of helplessness – a kind of silent anguish – was, I

35

now realize, my prayer. God was reading in my troubled heart the words and thoughts I could not myself compose. I am sure many of you have also experienced feeling the need to pray but not knowing how. For my part, I know I must try to raise my mind and heart to God. It's trying to pray that is important – however much it may seem to be a failure. God sees our effort and is pleased with that.

It is also important that we should realize that at every moment, in spite of all our faults and weaknesses, God looks down on each of us with loving eyes, waiting for us to return to Him. The prophet Isaiah spoke to men and women who were in despair. They had said, "God has abandoned us, the Lord has forgotten us". The Prophet gives them this wonderful word from God:

Does a woman forget her baby at the breast,
or fail to cherish the son of her womb?
Yet even if these forget,
I will never forget you.

We have the assurance then of the unshakeable love of God for each of us, in His promise never to forget. As we reflect on a day when we have all heard much about allied bombing raids, and the grim reality of war has been borne in on us, we must not forget those whose lives are directly touched by the unfolding events in the Gulf.

So let us pray for families and friends, anxious about their loved ones bravely playing their part in the conflict; we pray, Lord, that You will comfort and support them during the difficult times that lie ahead; we pray for all those in the armed forces, the medical workers and those who care for the casualties on both sides, that the horrors of war may inspire good deeds, unselfish love and a longing for the ways of God rather than hatred

36

and bitterness. We pray, too, for the victims of war, on either side, that You will welcome those who die into Your eternal and loving care, and that the injured may know Your healing touch. Finally, we pray for our leaders who carry the heavy responsibility of taking decisions in this war. Grant them wise judgement and moral courage and help them to act to bring lasting peace to the Gulf, based on justice and truth.

All these prayers, Lord, we commend to You this night. In Your great love for each one of us give us peace in our hearts, protect our loved ones, guide our leaders. Help us to hope and to trust, to trust that out of this sad and difficult conflict something better and more pleasing to You may emerge.

Basil Hume

3

Images

The Prisoners

The sight of prisoners of war, mouthing the words they were forced to speak, has sent the first ripples of real anger around the world. The Iraqi horror video made me shiver with anger – but also with fear.

War is always, and inescapably, a descent into barbarism. The attempt to impose rules on the conduct of war is an attempt to maintain at least a crust of civilization over the erupting horrors of destruction and death.

It's particularly the treatment of prisoners, those most vulnerable casualties of war, which tells us whether that thin crust of civilization is still in place. Iraq's treatment of the very first prisoners is like a jagged hole, an invitation to sink through it, deeper into barbarism.

Our treatment of prisoners will, I believe, remain just and good; but there are signs already in this morning's papers that our growing anger at Iraq may erupt in other ways. And I fear that belief in God may be neither true enough, nor strong enough, to hold us within the clear confines of justice.

Already I find myself wanting to make God a prisoner of my own need and my own imaginings, to hear from

Him the words that I so urgently need to hear at the start of a war: words of comfort and of blessing, of approval, of reassurance that all will be well. But I know that God is not a prisoner of our war. He is the God of justice and of truth. And since this war began, I've found myself unable to say anything to God at all. I sit silent before Him, often in tears, partly because I wonder whether the God of justice, far from giving easy comfort, may in fact be angry with all of us: angry at the evil aggression which is the cause of this war: angry at the claims, from both sides, that a holy war – or a just war – is being waged in His name: angry at the perversion of intelligence and skill being used to perfect weapons of war: angry because if the five months of intense planning, the resources, and a fraction of the money – just the money spent on day one of this war – had been put into the relief of famine, there would today be not one starving person in the whole of Africa.

If God is absolute love, then He is therefore also ultimate judge. If we want Him to speak easy words of comfort and peace, we shall hear neither. But because He is both truth and justice, if we hold to what is good and true, we may eventually find comfort: and if we seek and work for justice, then we may, in the end, find peace.

Philip Crowe

Hostages and Home

Only yesterday I was in Lincolnshire,
where there are many RAF families;
and I heard of one family
whose son had been posted "missing".

Then they had seen him amongst the televised
prisoners.
Whatever we may have thought, *they* were overjoyed.
He was alive
and I'm sure they heard clearly
almost the only authentic words on his lips,
when he asked for prayers
that he would be home again soon.

These are the two words I want to commend to you:
"Safe" and "Soon".
And often they add up to "home".

The First World War had a song,
"Keep the home fires burning",
which will be the job for most of us.
Whilst we wait and pray,
those in the Gulf will be praying
that at home you too are safe
and that they'll soon be back with you,
at home where they have known your love and
support –
Wives and children,
Mums and Dads,
Nans and Grand-dads,
Tonight we are one big extended family.

Here, or at your fireside,
waiting and hoping,
we pray for a just peace for all;
and, dear God,
keep our families safe and well
and have them home again soon.

Derek Worlock

The Cormorant

Last night the miracle of satellite television brought into my house a dying bird, a cormorant drowning in a sea of oil in far Kuwait. My heart, well defended against news of lost pilots and bombed cities, screamed in protest at the obscenity of a creature facing death alone on an alien shore. How strange and strong are the bunkers in which we shelter, eyes glued to news from the Gulf but hearts sealed in a locked room to keep out the terrifying gas of truth.

How long, I wonder, before that truth will creep under the door, behind the masking tape, to fill our lungs? When will we rush to the door to vomit, sick with the truth that each radiant firework that soars across the television screen brings death to those who are, in God's sight, our own kith and kin?

I pray that the sight of a dying sea bird may open doors which are barred against the screams of orphans and widows.

Sheila Cassidy

Designer and Weaver

In College chapel, we were saying the Psalms, and came across the line "God is the Lord who crushes wars". That piece of pious wishful thinking was the end of morning prayer for me. Whether in Lithuania, or in Northern Ireland, or in the Gulf, God does not intervene to prevent the tragic errors of human life. Manifestly He does not crush wars.

Far from intervening in miraculous ways, God seems more often, even to those who believe in Him, to be absent altogether. Jesus Himself cried out in the words of another Psalm during the crucifixion, "My God, My God, why did You forsake Me?" When God seems to be absent, when everywhere in the world is heard the sound of things breaking, it's hard to hold to the belief that the God of the resurrection is still creating life out of death, good out of evil.

In a small part of the Middle East, they use a time-honoured way of making exotic, fabulously expensive carpets. The canvas is suspended vertically from the ceiling to the floor. The designer sits on one side, the weavers on the other. It's the designer who has the piles of beautifully coloured wool, and the pattern is on both sides. He threads the wool through the canvas to the weavers, who carefully thread it back, working with the designer and with one another as together they develop a work of patient and beautiful craftsmanship.

But if they don't: if, for whatever reason, the weavers fail to work with the designer or with one another, what then? If the designer is not up to the job, there's chaos. But if the designer is sufficiently skilful, then he takes the wool, wherever they push it through the canvas, and threads it back to the weavers in a way which not only invites and encourages them to work with him again, but also at the same time continues to develop a pattern.

To believe in the God of the resurrection is to cling to the hope, against all the odds, that God will bring life out of death, and order, even out of chaos.

Philip Crowe

43

The Stranger

He was barely visible in the starlight. Perhaps that was the trouble from the start. Maybe if we'd been able to see him properly... well, anyway we couldn't. As far as we were concerned, he was a real threat. He might have seen us as we crept along the ridge; raised the alarm and shot the three of us to hell.

Not that that would have made much difference. Perhaps we would have preferred that.

As I was saying, we crept along, belly down, heart thumping, palms sweating. They say you're not frightened when it comes to the real thing. Well, I was. I was as frightened as hell. Mouth dry, stomach in knots, knees like jelly. The way the Major had looked at us when he gave us our orders had started it. It wasn't pity or sympathy or anything like that. More like the look of someone who's saying goodbye – for the last time. "Goodbye, old son. Nice knowing you. See you in hell some day, I expect." That kind of look. It kept coming back to me – now, for Pete's sake, when every movement, every detail was supposed to require all concentration I could muster.

It hadn't been too bad at the start. The CSM had dropped us about a mile back, at the foot of this long, gentle ridge. It was cold – and wet under foot. Funny in a desert, that. But we had been able to half-whisper to each other; the odd wisecrack, the occasional curse as we stumbled, the inevitable moan and groan about "just our blooming luck" to get lumbered with a mission like this.

When we got near the top of the ridge, Sam, the Lieutenant, only you would not know because on a caper like this it's all first names and you take people as you find them in the thick of it... Sam signalled absolute silence as we tried to look over the dead ground

44

behind the ridge. I couldn't see a thing. Not a thing. But as we waited for Sam to have a good look through his night-vision binoculars, I did begin to be able to distinguish one fold of hill from the next. But that was all. I was so cold that...

I felt Sam tense up. He was frozen still. Not a muscle moved. Not a flicker. Then in slow motion he passed me the binoculars, indicating where I should look. At first nothing. Empty red-flared desert in the weird light of the night-visions. I began to wonder if Sam was seeing things, going to pieces... It happens. He's even younger than me... Then I saw him. He was crouched down. it was a funny posture. Not like the Arabs I've seen at the base, turned to Mecca, praying with their behinds in the air. Not kneeling like we might kneel, either. Just crouched. Withdrawn, almost. And still. He must have put his rifle down on the ground. Good: that gives us a couple more seconds. I could see his uniform, even make out the flashes on his shoulder. Know it anywhere, by now of course. I must have looked at him for a couple of minutes, and not a move. But he couldn't be asleep. Not like that.

Pete nudged me and I passed him the binoculars. He watched for what seemed like hours. Sam made a sign, the sign. It said simply, "Go and get him with your knife while we cover you. And don't make a sound or I'll kill you with my bare hands."

Course, he knew that this is the one thing I can do better than any of them. Every training session we'd had together, it was always the same. Sam the long-distance marksman. Pete the tracker. And me... me the close-up killer. So that's what was wanted now. It had to be me.

He was only five hundred yards away. At most. But I'll swear it was the longest five hundred yards of my life. No cover. Loose stones that you couldn't help kicking. And dark. I couldn't see him. I knew pretty well where he was, but I wasn't going to clutter myself up with binocs for a job like this. I'd get within twenty yards and listen. He'd be bound to make a sound sooner or later. Then I'd have him. Nearly.

It was slow, so slow. Not slow enough, it seems now. But, though I says it as shouldn't, I moved well. Barely a sound. Good, that. I knew the others would realize it would take a time. I wasn't worried about them. Just get a little bit nearer... As I expected, I heard him. A deep sigh, almost a groan, even a sob. And then a few words muttered to himself. And then absolute silence again. Maybe he has gone to sleep, I thought. Great.

The knife went in easy, like it always does. He must have realized in the last split second, as my hand closed over his mouth. I could feel him go rigid. Then everything seemed to go slack.

I felt for his wrist pulse, to make sure. My hand strayed over his palm. Odd. I grabbed the other palm. Oh God!

Hardly knowing what I was doing, careless of sound or anything else, I pulled his soft sandals off his feet. Yes. Yes. The great gaping holes matched each other perfectly.

I didn't need to look at his side. I knew it. Almost mechanically I pulled at his uniform to show Sam and Pete. I didn't need to know. I didn't want to know any more. Just a skellick of uncertainty, or ambiguity... please, God, please. Leave me that, can't You?

But He couldn't.

Hilary Elliott

46

War Words

"Live from the Gulf",
reporting death
the language shifts,
the tangle of missiles and machinery are "kills",
"casualties" disguises the torn flesh and corpses;
"carpet bombing" blankets the pain
of high explosives wiping the ground
clean of all that lives and breathes and grows.

"Live from the Gulf",
to rehearse an orchestrated war-dance
in the suburban lounge,
to milk the adrenalin
as Patriot smashes Scud
and the anonymous bleeding figure
is stretcher-borne, repeat after repeat,
past the camera crew.

The theatre of war
has become the video,
vicarious vehicle of outrage,
designed to fuel allied determination.
The ambivalent signal cannot be contained.
Designed for Western Screens
the dew of its communication falls,
corrosive acid, on the dignity of other cultures
and the million neglected victims of the famine war.

"Live from the Gulf",
watching, the woman felt the assault
on the compassion
she'd spent her life to build
with healing caress and the reassurance
of encircling arms.

For a moment the temptation welled
to smash, revenge the damage,
then she reached to embrace the unquiet world
and hush it into harmony.

Michael Hare Duke

The Cup of Priorities

We ploughed the fields of Europe, and scattered
  deterrent missile silos.
Now we furrow the desert with explosions.
We shall harvest body bags.

We took a desert and drank oil from it.
Now we shall distil blood.

We cut the technological cards
And will draw wounds.

We, too, are to be ploughed and our pride scattered.
Our brows furrowed,
Our priorities in bunkers.

The priorities we proposed have come under the
  Scythe of Time
and the Plough of Events.
What will grow in these desert furrows.
If the oil burns, what shall we drink?

There are two cups lying here
From one, we drink bitterness and death – we drink it
  against ourselves.
From the other, we drink peace and hope – we drink it
  for ourselves.

In the last day, when we drink our life to its dregs,
   and there is no more,
it will matter which cup we drink.
How do we know which cup is which?

There are not two cups.
Each is broken, and the pieces lie together.
The pitcher is broken at the fountain.
One cup of God is broken at the oil-well, the other at
   the fountain of blood, and of human courage.
All the fragments are in our hands.
It is painful.

Yet, pain is life.
The living fragments, the atoms of Christ's love are
   present here and mingle with the fragments of our
   disturbed minds and bodies. All our betrayals are
   swallowed up in the one betrayal.
"Father, forgive them, for they know not what
   they do."

Let us look again at our priorities.

Iain Mackenzie

The Bitter Cup

Dear God, with You everything is possible. Let this cup
of war, killing and destruction, this cup of bloodshed,
human anguish and desolation, this cup of torture,
breakage in human relationships and abandonment
…Dear God, let this cup pass us by.

We are afraid. We are trembling in the depth of our
being. We feel the sweat and tears of thousands of

49

people all over the world, people who are afraid – afraid
to fight, afraid to kill, afraid of being killed, afraid of an
uncertain future.

Please, dear Lord, let this cup pass us by.

But, dear Lord – and we say this with the same trust as
Your Son, Jesus – not our will, but Your will be done.
We look ahead and see only darkness. We look around
and see only despair. We so much want our desire to be
the same as Your will, but when You call us to walk
through this valley of tears and darkness, help us to be
faithful, faithful to the end.

Protect our hearts from bitterness, resentment, and
the desire for revenge; keep our hearts close to the
heart of Jesus who was willing to die for us and so give
us new life.

As we pray, speak to us in the depths of our being and
remind us that, whatever happens in this dark world,
we are and remain Your blessed daughters and sons.

Henri J M Nouwen

A View from Wincobank, Sheffield, in Time of War

You can almost see the factory from here –
a few miles down the valley of the Don –
where that tube was forged
that might have turned into a supergun
aiming shells towards its maker's sons.

Look the other way –
high up towards the moors,
in those wooded valleys
the arrowheads were sharpened – so they say –
that won us Agincourt.

Who knows if the injuries
inflicted round this hill
from the vantage of this ancient fort
(dated, ironically, in the Iron Age,
oldest known human settlement hereabouts,
on whose ramparts I now stand)
reverberate in our deeds today,
the actions of our ancestors
visited yet upon us,
to the umpteenth generation?

Steadily to look and so remember
is to feel the ambiguities of war,
and run the risk of being shouted down
by those simplicities that betray humanity.
But such a contemplation is the prelude to a prayer
that is not cheap or blind.

And in the silence as we look and listen,
questions rise to form the substance of that prayer.

How do we contain the violence that lashes out
   in vengeance?
How limit the excitement of the fight?
How restrain the tyrant who builds a fearsome
   arsenal?
How keep the bully's hands off weapons biological,
   and chemical, and nuclear?
In whose hands dare we place the arms we
   manufacture?

What price the rule of international law?
Peace-keeping forces of police replacing armies old?
The banning of the trade in arms for profit?
(As we do the dust that poisons children's veins.)
Offensive weapons kept under international control?
Defensive weapons alone allowed to national
    governments?
Is the price a loss of national pride and regimental
    colours?

Is the first duty of government the defence of the
    realm?
Or resolving human conflicts without slaughter?
Or protecting our planet from those who would
    destroy it?

The questions press insistently
and need to take up residence in our heart,
to be held there steadily in our prayer.

From within this fortress on a hill
a mound of grass has taken shape,
man's harshness gentled by a woman's touch.
We bear our questions, fortified by hope.

The prayer is willed
here upon this hill that saw a city bombed,
whose edges sharpened from the iron
have done their bit in cutting down the enemy...

Jim Cotter

Gulf

My sombre dictionary starkly states
and without compromise,
that the word means "dividing lines impassable",
"a depth without recall",
"hollows deepening to chasms",
and, more chillingly, "abyss".
And, as I watch the faces on my screen,
young freckled lads from Minnesota,
a nurse from Aberdeen,
and the dark eyes of a new-minted soldier, all of
    seventeen,
from East Baghdad,
I ache and ache.
What depth beyond recall lies in your deaths?
What impassable dividing line will then be breached
when we have split the heavens with our wars,
and with such holes rent in our skies, our hearts, our
    worlds,
what Gulf lies there for us?

Baa Hare Duke

4

Icons of Hope

Our Neighbour's Brother

Horror piles on horror on all sides in the Gulf War – the
cries of the wounded and despairing, the awfulness of
the oil slick bringing its own train of death and
destruction to marine life – I found myself filled with a
feeling of almost unbearable compassion at the sight of
a single beautiful bird trying to fight against the
overpowering tide of oil which inexorably conquered it
– and with it the implicit threat of pollution on a massive
scale to the desalination plants on which the very lives
of huge numbers of people depend – one is saturated
with horror. And as yet, we are told, much worse is still
to come.

Christians, and men and women of goodwill, are
divided on whether this is or is not a just war, but
already in our own country, inevitably perhaps, relations
between the communities, between the faiths, are
suffering and will, undoubtedly, suffer more. Inter-
faith harmony, inter-religious dialogue, those most
fragile of plants, have received the harshest of bruisings
– the Mosque at Woking is attacked, poor immigrant
families, already cruelly assailed, are firebombed, and
on the other side, the crudest Muslim fundamentalists
are shown preaching their own brand of perverted

fanaticism, forgetting completely the tragic fate of the
inhabitants of Halabjah, innocent victims of the
diabolical Saddam Hussein's diabolical chemical
weapons.

Where do we turn and what are we to believe? Perhaps
we need icons of hope – images through which we can
see, even in these catastrophic times, evidence of God's
presence in His world. I have two, to which I cling – the
gentle humanity and quiet wisdom of Professor Rowan
Williams, and the sight on television of John Simpson,
the BBC's correspondent in Baghdad, being warmly
embraced on his expulsion from Iraq, by his Iraqi
minder. If two men on opposing sides can yet overcome
the belligerence of their countries, surely it is imperative
that those of us who live in peace and security in this
country should commit ourselves steadfastly to the
principles of racial and religious harmony – we are still
our neighbour's brother.

Nadir Dinshaw

A Very Great Hope

I am sure that the mood in Britain is quite different
from the mood at the time of the Falklands conflict. At
the beginning of last week there was a feeling of
impotence, as diplomatic effort failed. It was rather
like being children – electing our governments and
then waiting to see if the adults would decide for life or
for death. Now that there is war, I sense that there is
not the degree of triumphalism, gung-ho as we say –
rather the following of deliberate policy in a professional
way.

This was illuminated for me by a colleague who said:
even in a war whose justice is most clearly apparent,

there is always sin. And, I sense that we understand more fully what we are doing – have a greater humility, if you like.

At the outbreak of hostilities, Cardinal Basil Hume said that his first reaction was to go and pray. It was mine too. And I notice that the Prime Minister has several times referred to prayer. So it might be as well to know what we're up to when we pray. Prayer isn't to manipulate God, use God as a divine warranty for the benefit of what we want and **our** public relations. As a great Christian woman said – prayer is a piece of **work**, a costly self-surrender to God for the work **He** wants done on other people, on situations like the Gulf.

So, if you've felt the need to pray over these past days, like Mr Major or Cardinal Hume, the **way** of prayer (I use the word with real emphasis) is threefold:

- to offer your own faith and love and readiness to hold to God come what may
- to offer your own faith that God **is** present and active in the world and in the life of the person or situation to be prayed for
- and to offer yourself as an instrument of God.

It isn't infantile to pray for peace, or for our Forces, or for the Kuwaitis or the Iraqis. What we're doing is struggling to focus love on a collection of people, a situation, a place – so that the fullness of God's presence is increased.

Beyond our prayers, the Bible offers great visions of peace, those prospects of rural calm and prosperity held out by the prophets. And to dream such dreams of real peace and freedom is all but to weep. Because it seems all but possible – just out of reach. And, in other ways, further away than the furthest star. We're stuck, and to use an Americanism, we don't know how the hell to get out of it. And that's right because hell is the place you can't get out of. But, as I understand the Christian religion, God is in hell. He descended there, we say. And that's where we meet Him, come to know Him. And I suspect that people have been floating into churches because they sense that Christ is a way out of it, an alternative way, a way of peace, a way of prayer for the miraculous to happen. You've heard it all before. It's so hard to say it in a way that makes it real, makes it happen. Nation shall not lift up sword against nation, neither shall there be war any more – so goes the dream.

And that is our hope. It is our only hope. That's what religion is about if it's about anything that really matters.

So, if your mood has been anything like mine in past days, it's a mixture of despair and hope. And if I may say so, I shouldn't worry about the mixture. Despair and hope travel on every road we take. Despair at our warring madness. Hope in Him who travels with us and for us. And it's a very great hope as hopes go. Because nothing can prevail against Him – nor death, nor the hell of war. Nothing can be the end of Him or of the mystery and majesty of His love.

Colin Semper

Sitting with it

I go apart to pray, and feel a resistance even before I have tried. I know I will have difficulty praying about this war. I don't know how to begin.

When I intercede for a troubled person, I visualize holding her in my arms before God – until God stretches

58

out to take her from me: then I can step back and leave her where the love and strength are a billion times greater than mine...

But I can't hold this war: when I try, everything and everyone caught up in its vast network spills out of my arms. It is too hot – and too huge – to handle. I arrive before God and am empty-handed. No prayer wells up in me – just horror and helplessness. And then – tears.

At first I am ashamed. The tears go on and on. Not much of my praying is saying these days: none the less I feel I ought now to have some words to offer.

And then slowly it comes to me that just "sitting with it"... being struck dumb and shedding this fountain of tears... is not a failure to pray. Being horrified and helpless and sad and frightened and spiritually smashed up in the presence of God... feeling in every cell, as it were, the pain, violence, futility and guilt of war... maybe this, of itself, is prayer.

And I stay with that for a while.

Then something else comes. The conviction that, having sat in the mud, I can maybe now lift my eyes to the stars. In the past, prayer has taken me beyond the "is" of a situation to the "what has not yet come to be". Might it not do so now?

If I am stuck for ever at the point of helplessness and grief, then perhaps I am blocking the channels for God's love to become the mighty rushing wind of change. Prayer is a protest against the "human inevitable", and a standing up for "God's possible".

I move to focus on the love of God, the peace and justice and integrity of God, the Kingdom of God – and suddenly I find I can bear this war in my arms and heart... Just for a fraction of a second.

For the moment, there is nothing more I can do – except take something of this furnace of love with me and try to let it live, in little sparks and flickers, wherever and with whomsoever I may be. Not letting the helplessness have the upper hand. Maintaining hope. Not giving up on God's "yet to come". Being some sort of parable – however puny – of the "shalom" God wants for the world.

Kate Compston

A Glint of Humour

Optimism need not depend on the swingometer of the news. We can choose it. In the first hours of the war one had to pinch oneself to remember this was real. Precisely because – yet – we haven't seen the stomach-churning horrors of war films like A*pocalypse Now* or *The Killing Fields*, we have been able to enjoy this as entertainment. I mean, could Walt Disney or Spielberg have done better than the Tomahawk missiles speeding down the Baghdad dual carriageway? Yes, of course, in Disney it would have knocked on the correct door before exploding.

It has palled, of course. The richest diet palls, indeed, the richer, the sooner, and now we're wondering if we have the stomach for this media long haul. Yet, without it we would not know even the limited amount we do know.

And you can argue that the entertainment aspect, the style of media presentation, has its own healing component. It's a nice balance. Some will say it conceals the true horror, others that it midwifes the unacceptable reality acceptably into our homes.

Despite apocalyptic pessimists, I've never stopped believing that the human race is evolving. Just as modern precision surgery can save limbs and lives where surgeons of not so long ago could only chop off and hope for the best, so the development of state of the art technology in weapon systems could – I only say could – lead gradually to the end of indiscriminate catastrophes like Dresden and Hiroshima. It does at least extend the range of what we are these days pleased to call "options". We are in so many ways a brilliant species, and there is a grace in so much of what we do that inspires and – yes – entertains even as this war threatens to escalate in horror.

The dry humour of John Simpson in a position of danger, being asked by David Dimbleby, "John, where are you getting all this information?", and John replying, "I've been listening to your programme, David." The grace of a British tornado pilot, his cheeky face lined with fatigue, saying, "When I'd hit the target, my concern was how to run away bravely." The grace of the Israelis, accepting for the second time in a century that they be herded into sealed rooms *and* the grace of at least some Iraqis, who, under severe pressure, continued to treat British and Americans pleasantly. All this contrasts with many of those who still plead for peace. Why are so many of them *un*grateful, pompous, petulant and humourless? Frustration, passion, a sense of horror, no doubt. But if they are to win converts to their important arguments, they will need a little more of what Christians call Grace. Love does not contort its face in rage; a concerned faith does not exclude hope. And, as those in the *front* line are reminding us, good humour is a form of hope.

Iain Mackenzie

Kneeling Before the Dogs of War

A dreadful noise only yards from my home drew my eyes from the altar of war on television. I was energised:

first alarmed, then entertained, and finally moved to silence.

Dogs fighting caused the alarm. Not dogs as metaphors, but the four-legged kind. A Rottweiler had tangled with a sheepdog, held by a frightened woman. The Rottweiler's mate, an Alsatian, ran up and down in excitement. The attacker's owner, a man I know, who usually has them under exemplary control, was distressed. After the sound of battle had raged hither and thither, the sheepdog and its mistress made good their escape. The man looked up and down the street. It was empty. He did not realize that I could see him from my upstairs window. He kneeled. For ten minutes at their eye level, he talked earnestly to them, as they gazed into his eyes. Then he released them for their regular release of energy in the wild ground opposite.

Is this, I pondered, how God kneels before us? I went and sat comfortably before my TV war. But no, not this. War cannot be what our brilliance and beauty as a species is designed for. Surely, not only, or mainly, for this, our bravery, humour, capacity to bond and set free. But if not for war, then for what? Peace can be so boring! Must the zest for adventure always be repressed, sublimated, turned inwards? Or are we meant to go much further out in exploration, not to colonise, but fructify the wild universe? First, however, we have to make our planet less wild. Or... perhaps we will only have the perspective to do that when we see it from afar, in its paradisal fragility. Then, our descendants may kneel in the fields of stars and talk to the dogs of war in such a way that they, with the lamb and the lion, will lie down together.

Iain Mackenzie

5

Words Before Prayer

Lament from Africa

My God, my God, why have You forsaken me?
Our God, our God, why have You forsaken us?
My God, our God, my Father, our Father
When will we ever learn, when will they ever learn?

Oh when will we ever learn that You intended us for
Shalom, for wholeness, for peace,
For fellowship, for togetherness, for brotherhood,
For sisterhood, for family?
When will we ever learn that You created us
As Your children,
As members of one family,
Your family,
The human family –
Created us for linking arms
To express our common humanity.

God, my Father,
I am filled
With anguish and puzzlement.
Why, oh God, is there so much
Suffering, such needless suffering?
Everywhere we look there is pain

And suffering.
Why must your people in El Salvador,
In Nicaragua,
In Guatemala,
In.........,
In.........—
Why must there be so much killing,
So much death and destruction,
So much bloodshed,
So much suffering,
So much oppression, and injustice, and poverty and
    hunger?

Why, oh why, my God, our God,
My Father, our Father,
Why must Your people endure all the mindless violence
And bloodletting in Ulster, in Ethiopia, in
the Sudan, in Somalia, in Liberia, in Angola, in
Mozambique, in South Africa, in......
In......

Oh God, my God, our God, my Father, our Father,
Please is there some explanation
For what is happening in the Lebanon –
Poor Terry Waite and those other hostages –
Can you tell me, please, why in
The land of the Prince of Peace, why
Should Your people suffer so in
Gaza, in the West Bank, in Beit Sahur,
From deportations, house demolitions and now
In Tel Aviv from Scuds,
Ever fearful of poisoning in chemical warfare?

I don't understand, oh God, my God,
Our God, oh my Father, our Father,
Why, oh why, must there be so much

Pain and suffering in Your creation so very good
   and beautiful?
In Sri Lanka, in Calcutta, in Burma, in Kampuchia
Why are there boat people bobbing
About so vulnerably between vile camps in Hong Kong
   and in the deep blue sea, and Viet Nam?
And what about Latvia, and Lithuania, and Chernobyl?

I am dumbfounded
I am bewildered
And in agony –

This is the world
You loved so much that for it
You gave Your only begotten
Son, our Lord and Saviour Jesus Christ, to hang
From the Cross, done to death,
Love nearly overwhelmed by hate,
Light nearly extinguished by darkness,
Life nearly destroyed by death –
But not quite –

For love vanquished hate
For life overcame death, there –
Light overwhelmed
Darkness, there –
And we can live with hope.

Now there is the carnage
And devastation in Iraq, in Kuwait, in Saudi Arabia,
   in Tel Aviv,
What am I to make of it all?
Why did Saddam attack and overrun Kuwait?
I don't know –
Why did America
Attack Granada, and go into Panama?

Why did Israel occupy the West Bank?
I don't know.

All I know, God, is that it's all so horrendous,
The high-tech war with computers
That declare that we are so advanced,
And we can bomb with breathtaking
Precision and people die and
Buildings collapse, and blood flows, whether it
Is precision-bombing or –
It is all the same, you are dead.
And in Paris, and New York, and Birmingham,
In Tel Aviv, in Baghdad, in Riyadh,
A mother waits anxiously for news
Of her son, of her daughter, of her husband.
A child waits......

In the Eucharist as we offer the bread
That bread is all the bewilderment, the anguish, the
    blood, the pain, the injustice,
The poverty, the hate, the anger, the fear, the death,
The war, the bombs –
And we offer it all together with
The perfect all self-sufficient sacrifice
Of the Lamb without blemish
For peace,
For transfiguration, for compassion,
For Bush, for Hussein, for soldiers,
For civilians, for peace, for Shalom,
For family, for togetherness –

Oh my God, our God, oh my Father,
When will we ever learn?
When will they ever learn?

Desmond Tutu

My Country...

Some people say: "My country is always right."

Some people say: "My country is always wrong."

Some people say: "My country is sometimes right and sometimes wrong but my country right or wrong."

To stick to one's country when one's country is wrong does not make the country right.

To stick to the right even when the world is wrong is the only way we know of to make everything right.

We call barbarians people living on the other side of the border.

We call civilized the people living on this side of the border.

We the civilized, living on this side of the border, are not ashamed to arm ourselves to the teeth so as to protect ourselves against barbarians living on the other side.

And when the barbarians born on the other side of the border invade us, we do not hesitate to kill them before we have tried to civilize them.

So we civilized exterminate barbarians without civilizing them.

And we persist in calling ourselves civilized.

Peter Maurin

The Last Word

God is infuriating, because God insists on having the last word.

There have been a lot of words spoken since Saddam Hussein invaded Kuwait: angry ones, hurt ones, words of disbelief, of persuasion, of diplomacy. All of them intended to prevent war. And in the early morning of

16 January they failed. God, it seems, did not have the last word.

There were a lot of words spoken during the first Holy Week: Pilate's word of careful caution, "I can find no fault in this man"; Caiaphas' word of skilful blackmail, "You are no friend of Caesar's if you let this man go"; Peter's word of tawdry betrayal, "I've never seen the man in my life"; and the angry words of the crowd, whipped up into a frenzy, "Crucify Him! Crucify Him!" And when you get the words of a cautious politician, joined to the words of a compromised churchman, allied to the words of a disloyal friend, drowned by the shouts of a hostile mob, then that's a pretty powerful combination.

But the infuriating thing about God is not just that He insists on having the last word, but He doesn't seem to mind if nobody hears it. So God's last word on Holy Week wasn't spoken where it could be heard by the powerful, or the compromised, or the disloyal or the angry, but in the dawn silence beside yesterday's grave. And to hear God's last word today, we'll need to listen not to the whine of the missiles or the eruption of the explosions or the droning of the aircraft or the sound of the guns, but to the faint echoes of struggling faith and flickering hope and patient love. There, God's last word will be saying what it once said beside yesterday's grave: that God has the last word over evil.

Evil works like a spiral. Bitterness provokes resentment, resentment begets hatred, hatred produces violence, violence results in escalating violence and so it goes on unless someone says, as Jesus said on the Cross, "Stop the spiral, I want to get off". "Father, forgive them..."

Edmund Burke once said that "the only thing necessary for the triumph of evil is for good men to do nothing". The Irish poet W B Yeats once wrote, "the

68

best lack all conviction, while the worst are full of passionate intensity". Over the years, stretching back to the beginning of this century, good men have tried to do something about the injustice in the Middle East, but too many good men have done nothing. There have been policies pursued which lacked any conviction save that of self-interest. And there has been too much passionate intensity on all sides.

There must have been a lot of good men who did nothing that first Holy Week. To be fair, they probably didn't realize they were caught up in anything as serious as evil. But then, we never do. Until it is too late. There must have been a lot who lacked conviction that first Holy Week, who could have done something to resist the creeping threat of evil. But to be fair, they probably thought someone else would. We always do. And so the worst, who were full of passionate intensity, appeared to win the day. Only those with a great deal of insight, or an abundance of grace, recognize that the greatest weapon evil has at its command is its ability to persuade us either to ignore it, or to accommodate ourselves to it, until it is too late. That is why Martin Luther King said to a society riddled with the evil of racism, "He who accepts evil without protesting against it is really co-operating with it", and why, when the nuclear scientist Robert Oppenheimer was asked what most occupied his thoughts, he replied, "the evil of humanity".

What happened on 2 August and the atrocities which followed the invasion of Kuwait, were evil. What happened on 16 January was evil. The fact that the coalition's actions are the lesser of two evils doesn't lessen the analysis. So let's not underestimate the power of evil, or minimize the ease with which we all unwittingly become embroiled in it. But don't forget that God has the last word over evil.

And God has the last word over suffering: the

suffering that we have seen and will go on seeing in the faces of captured airmen, and Iraqi civilians, and Israeli women running for shelter. To the person who asks where God was when his son was killed, Christian faith can only struggle to answer "where He was when His own son was killed", dying with the burning question, "My God, why?" Countless attempts have been made to answer that question. H G Wells spoke for many when he wrote that the Easter postlude was just a happy ending imposed by a sentimental editor on an essentially tragic story. And so it would have been if the risen Christ had not borne on His hands and side the imprint of the nails and spear. Suffering isn't removed by magic or explained away by logic, but a God who is in the suffering with us can transform it.

> The other gods were strong, but Thou wast weak,
> They rode, but Thou didst stumble to a throne.
> To our wounds only God's wounds can speak,
> And not a God has wounds, but Thou alone.

As we watch the television pictures of this first "media" war, we won't be tempted to underplay the power of suffering or underestimate its reality behind the brave face or smile. Families won't escape it. But God has the last word over suffering, as He absorbs it into Himself and transforms it.

And God has the last word over death. "This Jesus, whom ye crucified, God raised." That was the substance of the first Christian sermon, and it has been repeated down the centuries, because without Easter not a single word of the Christian Gospel would have survived. Maybe, without Easter, Jesus might have become the subject of the occasional tragic poem, but never the source of the Gospel.

Holy Week and Easter are about the reality and the

dream. We suppose the reality is Pilate's cynicism and Caiaphas' hatred and Peter's betrayal and the crowd's hysteria. We suppose the reality is missile-drenched cities, and innocent lives lost, and young men and women at war. The reality is cruel dictatorship and atrocity, the victory of evil and suffering, and death. And we suppose the dream is of evil ultimately losing, and suffering unable totally to destroy, and death finally defeated. But God's last word makes the reality a dream, and the dream a reality. God's last word makes it an illusion that evil conquers, and a shadowland where suffering destroys and a fantasy that death is the end. And so, even in the midst of this war, God will always be trying somewhere to speak His last word, and so trying to give us, to our surprise, "garlands instead of ashes, the oil of gladness instead of mourning, and the mantle of praise instead of our faint spirits."

Johnston Mackay

Our Fractured Spirituality

Christians in Britain are divided over the Gulf War, and the divisions cut across denominational lines. Some, probably the majority, consider the war to be just, but a regrettable necessity: others, while acknowledging the possibility, do not consider the Gulf conflict fulfils the necessary conditions of a Just War: a minority are pacifist and do not believe war can ever be justified.

As war is a matter of life or death, not only for combatants but also for innocent civilians, and as this particular war could easily spread beyond the Gulf and involve the use of nuclear weapons, it could be a matter of life or death for millions, could malform future generations through the genetic effects of radiation, and could threaten the survival of the human race. It is extraordinary that while Christian churches are divided on doctrinal beliefs, on which the majority of members are very vague, division of belief is permitted on the question of war, a belief on which millions of lives, and perhaps the survival of the human race, depend. It therefore seems fair to conclude that our Christian spirituality is badly fractured over the most fundamental question of life and of religion, and over the Scripture's clear prohibition "Thou shalt not kill".

I suggest that we use the fact of the Gulf War and our attitudes to it as a way of testing the nature of our own belief in God, and of our own spirituality.

We all tend to idolatry, to choose some created thing rather than God, whether it be wealth, health, status, success, self-gratification, self-importance, an ideology or a belief system, and to devote our lives to the preservation of this idol. As the Old Testament prophets warn, we become what we worship and are eventually devoured by our idols. Religious people are most in danger of the worst form of idolatry. To dedicate one's life to amassing a fortune is much less damaging than to do so and stick the label "God" or "God's will" on our endeavours. It is against such idolatry that the Old Testament prophets rage. "When you stretch out your hands I turn my eyes away. You may multiply your prayers, I shall not listen. Your hands are covered with blood, wash, make yourselves clean. Take wrongdoing out of my sight. Cease to do evil. Learn to do good, search for justice, help the oppressed, be just to the orphan, plead for the widow" (Isaiah 1:15-17).

To fasten the label "Just War" onto a conflict which is not just, is to practise idolatry, for it is sanctioning the war in God's name. However elaborate the church services or prolonged the vigils for peace, our prayers will not be heard. The fact that Saddam Hussein is also idolatrous, claiming God is on his side, does not make us any less idolatrous.

In spite of all the rhetoric by the US and ourselves about the righteousness of our cause, of the need to stand firm against aggression and all the other righteous labels we stick on the conflict, the truth is that we have gone to war because Saddam Hussein has threatened our Western financial interests, and not because we are champions of freedom, democracy, truth or of innocent victims, causes which we readily ignore or oppose if it suits our national economic interests. We did not rush to war to defend Namibia when South Africa defied the United Nations and the world court, occupied Namibia for decades, looting, terrorizing and using the country as a base for attacking neighbouring states. Then we favoured "quiet diplomacy". For years in the UN, America has blocked political settlements of the Arab-Israeli conflict. Saddam Hussein was a tyrant before he invaded Kuwait, but that did not prevent US and Britain from supplying him with the weaponry which he is now using against us.

Here is an imaginative exercise with which to test our own spirituality in general and our attitude to the Gulf War in particular:

Imagine there is a ring on your doorbell one evening, and on answering you find the visitor is the Risen Jesus Himself. "Look, I am standing at the door, knocking. If one of you hears me calling and opens the door, I will come and share a meal side by side" (Revelation 3:20). So imagine how you and the rest of the household would welcome Him. You might find yourself making ridiculous statements to the Lord of all creation like, "Do make yourself at home, Jesus". He does so. Now take a leap in your imagination to two weeks later. Jesus has accepted your invitation and He is still with you. How is it now?

"Jesus Christ, yesterday, today and the same forever", so He still has the same characteristics as in the Gospel accounts. He said once, "I have come not to bring peace but the sword, to set daughter against mother, daughter-in-law against mother-in-law, son against father", so there may have been a bit of tension over family meals in the last two weeks, perhaps some leaving the table and banging the door as they left the room, or even the house, never to return.

You asked Him to be at home with you, so He has begun to invite His friends. The Pharisees complained that He dined with tax collectors and sinners. What kind of people are arriving at your house, what are the neighbours saying, and what is happening to the property values in the area?

You may have felt in the course of the fortnight that it was not right for you to keep Jesus all to yourself, so you arrange for Him to visit the local church, where He gives an address to a gathering of the devout, men and women. In the gospels He tells a gathering of scribes and Pharisees, "The tax gatherers and the prostitutes will get into the kingdom of God before you". He gives the same message at the parish church, causing uproar and the parish's loss of its principal benefactors.

You return home with Jesus and you have a problem on your hands, for life is becoming impossible, but Jesus is Lord of all creation and you can't throw Him out. You look around the house, find a suitable cupboard, clean it out and decorate it, sparing no expense, get a good strong lock on it, put Jesus inside, place flowers in front of it and bow reverently each time you pass. You now have Jesus in your home but He does not interfere or upset any more, so we can sit before the TV and watch the progress of the Just War in peace, thankful to hear that it is progressing satisfactorily "according to our game plan", that our weapons are hitting their targets and inflicting heavy damage.

But the Risen Lord cannot be confined to cupboards. He can reach to the very depths of our consciousness. "I love all that I have created. My living Spirit is in all. I gave My life out of love for every single human being. As you do to another, no matter who it may be, you are doing to Me, and you are also doing to yourself. I give you My peace, a peace that is risky, costly and comes through My wounded hands and side. Do you accept My peace?"

"As you enter a house, salute it, and if the house deserves it, let your peace descend upon it; if it does not, let your peace come back to you. And if anyone does not welcome you, or listen to what you have to say, as you walk out of the house or town, shake the dust from your feet. I tell you solemnly, on the day of Judgement it will not go as hard with the land of Sodom and Gomorrah as with that town" (Matthew 10:12-15).

Gerard Hughes SJ

Anxiety

There is the ever-present anxiety of those whose loved ones are serving in the armed Forces – an anxiety now alas in some cases turned into grief. There is the anxiety of not knowing, of wondering how much has not been told us. And for some there is the anxiety of knowing too much, the anxious burden carried by those who make the decisions, and who, like the armed Forces and their families, need our prayers.

Then, as we look to the future, there are anxieties about a possible escalation of the war. Is there a willingness to go on showing restraint? to go on fighting it by methods which demonstrate that restraint? and to stick to the main and limited objectives?

There are anxieties about the future of the area. How long will it take to restore trust and goodwill? Is it ever going to be possible to build a stable peace in the Middle East, and is war the right way to do it? These last two days have sharpened anxieties about irreparable damage to the environment. And here in Britain there is anxious concern about what the war may do to community relations. We mustn't fall into the trap of imagining that this is in any sense a war between the Muslim world and the West; still less between Islam and Christianity.

But deeper than all these grounds for anxiety there is in many of us, I suspect, a gnawing anxiety about war itself. No matter how right and inevitable the political decision to go to war – and I believe it was right – there is something in the Christian conscience which revolts against the whole idea. ·

"How blest are those of a gentle spirit: they shall have the earth for their possession... How blest are those who show mercy: mercy shall be shown to them... How blest are the peacemakers: God shall call them His sons..."

The words of Jesus confront and convict us. For Christians there is no escape from the dilemma they pose. On the one hand we want a world of justice where people can live in peace and security. On the other hand we seem driven to kill people in order to attain it. On the one hand we acknowledge the realities of power, and the dreadful consequences of either wielding it wrongly ourselves, or ignoring those who abuse it. On the other hand we believe that God is love, and long to conduct our affairs as if love were the only effective power.

It is a dilemma as old as faith itself, but the anxiety

76

it evokes can still tear us apart. There is no easy Christian answer to war.

Yet we are not left to bear all these anxieties alone. The very fact that the deepest of them lie in the heart of faith itself, can give some comfort and reassurance. Others besides ourselves have faced these dilemmas. Isaiah, in the passage just read to us, was struggling to find an answer to them six hundred years before Christ. God understands, He was saying. God wants to show pity. "The Lord is a God of justice. Happy are all who wait for Him."

Deal with your anxieties, in other words, by putting them in the context of God's purposes. Believe that in the long run justice will prevail. Don't be afraid to do what you believe is right because, despite awful tragedies, in the end this is a moral universe. Under the waves and turmoil on the surface of the sea runs the strong tide of God's goodness. "Happy are all who wait for Him."

That's one way of coping with anxiety – patience and trust. But there is another way, in those words "gentleness", "mercy" and "peace", which so stab at our consciences in time of war. The Jesus who spoke them is also the Jesus who lived by them. And the God He reveals to us is the God who deals gently with us, because He knows our frailties; the God who is merciful to us, and who judges us not in anger but in love; and the God whose peace can "stablish, strengthen, settle" us, as the prayer puts it, despite the anxieties which so threaten and disturb us.

To believe that God is like this, a God of gentleness, mercy and peace, doesn't actually cure anxiety. We shall go on worrying about war. And rightly so. There is a lot to worry about.

But although we cannot know what is coming, we know who is there already. God is not aloof from the

77

whole sorry mess in which we find ourselves. He is bearing the weight and the pain of it; in reaching out to Him as we do in an act of worship, we are enabled to bear some of the weight and pain of it with Him. And this can begin to transform anxiety. Instead of being a crippling burden centred on ourselves, it can become part of the loving concern, for each other and for His world, which we share with God.

John Habgood

Courage

Every human occupation or condition has its appropriate virtue. For nurses it is kindness. For politicians it is wisdom. And for warriors it is courage. Courage is the supreme military virtue. It is needed by those who face death or the prospect of terrible injury.

Courage is not fearlessness. There are human beings who seem to lack fear. They have fewer or stronger nerves than the rest of us. The fearless do not need courage. It is the fearful who need courage, because courage is the ability to deny your fear and do what has to be done. It takes courage to stand fast when every nerve in your body is telling you to flee.

Courage, then, is the virtue of the warrior. But there is more to courage than physical bravery. Moral courage is even more important, because it is needed all the time, whereas physical courage is needed mainly in war. There are two aspects of moral courage that we should note. First of all, it takes courage to stand against a prevailing idea or opinion. The pacifist who opposes war in the face of public enthusiasm for it, and the politician who calls for restraint in the way in which it is waged, both need courage.

78

And courage is needed in our search for truth. Most of us are content to believe what we are told by those in high places. It takes courage to question the received wisdom and to challenge those in power. This is sometimes called the heretical imperative. Those who follow this way are uncomfortable to live with. Their challenges to society usually bring derision upon their heads, sometimes even death. But they help societies cleanse and renew themselves.

The great women and men of faith are usually creatures of immense physical courage. In these days we need their examples before us and their words in our ears:

Be watchful, stand firm in your faith, be courageous, be strong.
Let all that you do be done in love.

Richard Holloway

Patience

Patience is a hard thing. It is a kind of suffering, a waiting and enduring. That is why we call sick people in hospital **patients**. They are suffering and they are being treated. This suggests that their role is entirely passive. They are not doing anything – they are being done unto. In short, they are **patients**, waiting for the treatment to end and healing to come.

All that it true enough, but something else has to be said. We know that patients in hospitals who are suffering from similar illnesses can heal at different speeds. This is because the quality of our patience or suffering has an effect on our whole nature. Attitude makes a difference. The way we wait, the way we endure, can be a positive fact that affects our well-being.

In this time of war the whole country is watching and waiting. We are all like patients waiting for health to be restored. Some wait with particular intensity, because they have loved ones who are on active service, missing in action or prisoners of war. That is the most demanding type of patience. One way to use this type of painful waiting is to turn it into prayer. To offer it, to endure it, for *them*. Prayer is a mysterious force, but it is a powerful one. Even people who don't believe in God pray. They *will* the health and well-being of others. They think lovingly of their friends, call them to mind. Who can tell what that activity of loving regard achieves? We are all part of one another, and when we pray we consciously pay attention to relationships we usually take for granted. Men and women of faith acknowledge all that, but there is something else they believe. There is One who is close to us all, especially in our suffering. When we draw close to Him we draw close to one another. That is why the Psalmist tells us:

Hold thee still in the Lord, and abide patiently upon Him.

Richard Holloway

6

Thoughts of Peace

Be Still and Know

Be still and know that I am God,
Be still and know.
At My command the planets wheel
And circle slow.

Be still and know that I am God,
Be still and know.
Beneath each chaos I am there,
The calm below.

Be still and know that I am God,
Be still and know.
How close the everlasting arms
Around you go.

Be still and know that I am God,
Be still and know.
I rule the tempest of the waves,
Their ebb and flow.

Be still and know that I am God,
Be still and know.
The deepest dark must yield itself
In daylight's glow.

Be still and know that I am God,
Be still and know.
Let every mouth my praises sing,
My glory show.

David Ogston

Peace is not...

Peace is not a thing to possess,
but a way of possessing;
Peace is not a gift to be given,
but a way of giving;
Peace is not a topic to teach,
but a way of teaching;
Peace is not a theory to learn,
but a way of learning;
Peace is not an opinion to hold,
but a way of holding;
Peace is not a resolution of strife,
but a way of striving;
Peace is not a creed to preach,
but a way of preaching;
Peace is not a God to serve,
but a way of serving;
Peace is not a question to ask,
but a way of asking;
Peace is not an answer to seek,
but a way of seeking;
Peace is not a journey's end,
but a way of journeying.

Richard Skinner

War and Peace

In the search for an answer to violence Christ has laid down standards to which Christians are called to respond. It becomes our duty to focus attention on those standards and to give them credibility by our allegiance. We may not be able to attain to anything like Christ's perfection, but we can at least strive towards that perfection, challenged by His love and encouraged by His grace.

A Meditation

...Let us reason together, saith the Lord – no annihilation without consultation.

...We trust the Holy Spirit in the great crises of life, but so often turn aside when war becomes "inevitable".

...Lord, what have You to say about the Gulf crisis, and are we willing to listen to Your Word?

...We do not know what war will do to the peoples of the Middle East; nor do we know what it will do to our own nation.

...What is a "human shield" – surely it is the innocent of every land?

...Lord, we know our earthly arithmetic – help us with the heavenly calculus.

...The money will be found for all-out war – when will the works of Love be given parity of esteem?

...Non-violent resistance to tyranny has not failed – it has not yet been fully tried.

..."Just War" philosophers – at the end of the day they leave us with *just* war.

...Is Christian witness possible with the Bible in one hand the "The Bomb" in the other?

...“Lord make me good, but not just yet” – the prayer
   of prevarication.
...When at the end of your tether, remember God is at
   the other end.

And from the bomb craters of Munich in 1944 comes this message of anguish and hope

O God, we do not understand where Your love has
gone: we do not understand where our own love has
disappeared. All that we experience, all that we know,
all that we see, is nothing but devastation, ruin, dust
and ashes. All that we feel is the shame in which we lie
helpless.

And yet we hear Your word: “I am the Resurrection
and the Life. He who believes in Me will not die, but I
will raise him up to eternal life.”

This is Your word, Lord. Pronounce it over our ashes.
Say it again over our corruption. Repeat it in power
over our failures.

The war-weary appeal of Father Erich Przywara
haunts us once again.

David Bleakley

Peace in the Jewish Tradition

There is a midrash which our Rabbis were very fond of
telling:

When the Children of Israel had miraculously crossed
the Red Sea and their pursuers met their watery death,
the Ministering Angels in heaven, like their human
counterparts below, were singing and dancing.
Gradually they noticed that God was quietly weeping.
They were puzzled and troubled and asked: “Are you

84

not pleased that Your children are saved and delivered from tyranny? Why do You not join in our celebration?" God replied: "How can I rejoice? My children are also drowning."

Our sages say: "Seek peace in your own place." You cannot find peace anywhere save in your own self. In the psalm we read: "There is no peace in my bones because of my sin." When a man has made peace within himself, he will be able to make peace in the whole world (Rabbi Simcha Bunam, Chassidic teacher (1765-1827)).

In the Jewish tradition there are 613 Commandments which comprise all the do's and don'ts derived from our Holy Scriptures. Of them 612 have their appointed times and places and men and women are expected to abide by them when they become actual. But there is one Commandment which is an exception to this rule. It is derived from the mandate:

"Seek peace and pursue it." To achieve peace you should anticipate it, run after it, and never cease to do all in your power to bring it about.

"Your first aim here on earth should be to be at peace with all men, Jew and non-Jew alike. Contend with no one. Your home should be a place of quietness and happiness, where no harsh word is ever heard, but love, friendship, modesty, and a spirit of gentleness and reverence rules at the time. But this spirit must not end with the home. In your dealings with the world you must allow neither money nor ambition to disturb you. Forego your rights in matters of honour, if need be, and above all envy no man. For the main thing is peace, peace with the whole world" (Rabbi Joel ben Abraham Shemariah, 18th Century, Vilnius, Lithuania).

Hugo Gryn

Whose Side?

Whose side is God on?

If we knew, we could perhaps make some sense of this war.

Saddam Hussein says Allah is on his side, so this is a holy war against "the infidels", that is, us.

King Fayd says Allah is on his side, so this is a holy war against a bad Muslim brother.

Sometimes voices have been heard claiming that this war is a crusade, the Christian version of the holy war.

But God is precisely the one who cannot be manipulated, exploited, used to confirm our own purposes.

So this cannot be a sacred war, a holy war, or a crusade.

It is a secular war.

If it is a secular war, then it falls within the scope of human liberty.

It is not like an earthquake or a volcano that make us ask: Why did God allow this?

This war is the result of a train of events set in motion by human choices, in which no one involved is exempt from guilt.

This war is the result of *miscalculations*, in the deepest sense of the word.

But the fact that God is on neither side does not mean that God is absent from the war.

God is on the side of those who suffer.

God is in the gore and the grime and the mangled bodies.

This war echoes the passion of Christ, the almighty one made vulnerable for us.

This war continues the passion.

This war is the passion.

"My God, my God, why have you abandoned Me?"

86

cried Jesus.

But He was not abandoned by God, not even in this moment of desolation.

Beyond the dark night of the passion glimmers the dawn of resurrection and a just peace.

If we believe that, we must work towards it.

To pray is to be committed.

Peter Hebblethwaite

Meditation on the Gulf Conflict

As news comes of bombs falling on Basra I find myself turning back to one of the founders of Islamic mysticism, Hasan Al-Basri, who died in AD 728: "The one who is contented and is without needs or cravings... will find peace... and the one who is patient for a short while will be prepared for Eternal Life."

Greed, envy and impatience are three components of the present crisis. One finds these tendencies on both sides of the violent engagement.

Energies that appeal for patience and forgiveness have been widely mobilized. Vigils and prayers have been offered in every known religious tradition. Enemy-image building must be checked, especially as it spreads from individuals to whole peoples, whole nations, whole religions. This, above all, is a time to pray for our enemies, as they share sufferings, often far greater than our own, to pray for all victims, military and civilian, young and old, and to pray for ourselves that the virus of greed and the virus of impatience and the virus of hatred may be checked.

John B Taylor

Outer Space

Viewed from outer space our planet Earth is a most beautiful place: swirling cloud, deep blue oceans, outline continents, deserts and mountains. Photographs show us all its splendour. It is beautiful to behold.

Those same photographs, if taken in the last few days, would reveal the most awful pictures: the heaviest, most consistent and devastating air bombardment and conflict now taking place in the Gulf.

Our popular images have always suggested that the view from outer space is somehow like God's view of our world. I'm sure that's not really true, for God is also described as closer to us than the air we breathe. But what do we see, if we step back, pause and wonder?

First of all we see a tragedy. Death and destruction is being spread across Iraq and Kuwait. Inevitably innocent people are dying. But then innocent people have been the victims ever since Kuwait was invaded. Has the full horror of that yet been revealed? This recourse to military action, in a different way, is a tragedy, too. It is so sad that our world has found no better way of settling this crisis. As the Pope has said, "This war diminishes humanity"; we are the poorer for it.

So our stance before God must be first of all one of seeking forgiveness. As the Psalmist says:

Have mercy on me, God, in your kindness.
In your compassion blot out my offence.
Oh wash me more and more from my guilt,
And cleanse me from my sin.
(Psalm 51)

Yet, in God's eyes, our world should be ordered, dignified, peaceful. Despite our sinfulness and despite the mess

88

we make of things, God does not withdraw His love. He wants us to find the right path, to know and cherish His design. He longs and longs for us to grow to the maturity and wisdom which would make war redundant. As the Lord Himself said:

> Look at the birds in the sky. They do not sow or reap or gather into barns, yet your heavenly Father feeds them. Are you not worth much more than they are? Set your hearts on the Kingdom first, and on God's saving justice, and all these other things will be given you as well. (Mark 6:26ff).

Only inasmuch as we learn to take God's view will we build the peace for which we long. In God's eyes every individual is to be respected. Human beings are not to be deceived, abused, tortured and killed.

Surely in God's eyes, too, nations are to live in peace, free to develop their history, culture and enterprise. And, in the view of the Creator of all, nations should know that they are but part of one world. They should willingly co-operate with each other, ready to meet the needs of the poorest, and prepared to uphold an international order through a body such as the United Nations.

Our prayers today must be for a quick end to this awful conflict. They must be for all involved in the fighting; for fearful anxious families, for the injured, the lost, the dead. We must pray that their sacrifice will not be in vain but that, in God's time, a true peace will be constructed.

Let God know that we are impatient for that to happen. But admit, in prayer, we cannot do it without His help.

That view from outer space makes clear not only the beauty of our earth, but also its fragility. Our greatness

is not our own: it comes from God, and God alone can
sustain it.

How great is your name, O Lord our God,
through all the Earth.

Vincent Nichols

Barakah

The Prophet Muhammad has absolutely no divine
attributes. Like Abraham and Moses he was a
Messenger. His life, his opinions, his actions all
demonstrate his essential humanity. He was a husband,
a father who wept at the premature death of his infant
child, a general, a legislator, a politician – he was a
man who grew in stature as he grew older, who could
be stern but also vulnerable; he valued learning and
accepted criticism when it was just, he enjoyed a joke
and was not pompous, he was firm in his faith without
being a fanatic, for he knew that there is no compulsion
in religion. For Muslims who pursue the spiritual path,
the Prophet Muhammad is the paradigm of mystical
sensibility. From this aspect of his personality,
epitomized by his Night Journey to heaven, flows the
authority for the profound religious illumination which
comes with *Barakah* or the grace of God. Each Muslim
who follows the example of Muhammad can embark on
his own journey. However, he must learn patience and
humility, he must submit to the will of God, he must
learn not only to find peace in prayer but to take joy in
it; to become sensitive, to listen, to distinguish certainty
from dogmatism, passionate commitment from anger.
The poem below attempts to reflect a little of this Islamic
Barakah.

90

To understand, to submit to the will of God
Is to welcome paradox, to stutter small truths,
To watch and wait, to tread lightly.

To understand, to submit to the will of God
Is to see frozen certainties melt, grow formless and
   new,
To sense senselessly, to touch without reward.

The Prophet, that snow-hearted man, avoiding
The conceit of analysis, received in darkness
Reluctantly, becoming an emptiness, an antithesis
A desert beyond space and time.

Rafriq S Abdulla

A Fragile Web

Peace is like gossamer –
vulnerable, yet indestructible:
tear it, and it will be rewoven.
Peace does not despair.
Begin to weave a web of peace:
start in the centre
and make peace with yourself
and your God.
Take the thread outwards
and build peace within your family, your community
– and in the circle of those you find it hard to like.
Then stretch your concern
into all the world.
Weave a web of peace
and do not despair.
Love is the warp in the fabric of life:
truth is the weft:

care and integrity together —
vulnerable
but ultimately
indestructible.
Together,
they spell
peace.

Kate Compston

7

Prayer into Action

Judging Justly

The Kurdish district of Garmiyan in the mountains of
north-eastern Iraq used to be a pretty place.

There were wheat fields and apricot orchards. The
gardens grew melons and pomegranates and grapes.
Most houses had a cow tethered outside.

One April morning in 1988, the mountainsides echoed
to the drone of Iraqi bombers and the flat thud of
chemical bombs. A white cloud drifted among the apricot
blossom. Whoever breathed it, died.

Later that day, a group of Kurdish guerrillas came
across a procession of people, blistered and burned,
stumbling silently from a stricken village.

Azad Abdulla was one of the guerrillas. "Can you
imagine", he asks, "what it's like to die this way? If it's
cyanide you get dizzy and choke. If it's mustard gas
your skin blisters and your lungs begin to bleed and
you drown in your own blood..."

Azad Abdulla and his companions found a small boy
and girl clinging to each other. While running away
through a wheat field they had come under attack from
an Iraqi helicopter and become separated from their
parents. The parents had died but the children did not
know this.

They kept saying that when it grew light they would go and look for them. They thought it was night, they did not realize that they were blind.

Almost to the day (on 12 April 1988), Junior Foreign Office Minister David Mellor was forecasting that British industry would soon find "a large market in Iraq".

Was he unaware that Saddam Hussein was systematically gassing Iraq's Kurdish minority? Hardly...

The world's inaction is a subject about which we at Amnesty International find it difficult to remain polite.

For years we have been exposing atrocities committed by the Iraqi government. Nothing effective has ever been done...

Yes, we told you so. In '80, '81, '82, '83, '84, '85, '86, '87, '88 and '89. And you did nothing effective to help...

"We were screaming till we could not speak," says Azad Abdulla, "and yet no one listened."

An extract from an advertisement of Amnesty International in the Independent, *17 November 1990.*

For Prayer

God of justice,

I find it hard to listen to those who are screaming for help,
because I want this conflict to go away and leave me in peace.

I find it hard to take effective action,
because I do not know what I should do.

If I support the war I am afraid that the killing will

escalate uncontrollably and the world suffer
irreversible environmental damage.

If I oppose the war I am afraid that I will be giving
victory to Saddam Hussein and so encouraging the
spread of his murderous regime.

If I oppose the war but support sanctions I am afraid
that I will be causing the suffering and death of
innocent civilians while leaving the oppressors
relatively untouched.

Give me ears to hear those who are crying,
clarity to weigh up the options,
generosity to decide what to do,
courage to carry it out,
humility to respect the decisions of others,
and perseverance to work for a long-term peace.

Take from us all
any hatred of the enemy,
any pleasure in destruction,
any glorying in battle,
any relish in victory.

Give peace to the world.
But until that comes,
give us in war
the peace that the world cannot give.

Margaret Hebblethwaite

International Justice

Our generation, as never before, has been profoundly affected by the enormous disparity in wealth between the countries of the rich northern hemisphere and the developing countries of the south. Modern communications technology has brought into our living rooms sights that in the past were hidden from our view.

The misery is no longer in faraway places. It has been brought home to us. The Brandt Report some years ago warned us that time was running out, and that even enlightened self-interest should lead developed countries to take radical action to redress the inequalities between north and south and to construct a more just world order...

Politicians tell us there are no votes in international aid. We should tell them they are wrong and that our vote would be given to enlightened policies aimed at alleviating the world's distress and injustice. We can and must still support our voluntary development and relief agencies. But we know that the problem can only be tackled by the nations working together...

The final horror of this century has been the appalling manifestation of man's inhumanity to man. There has been violent repression, blind hatred and inhuman cruelty. This is the century of the concentration camp and the Gulag Archipelago. This is the age of the Holocaust, when racial prejudice sanctioned the massacre of millions. This is an era of official torture and terrorist violence whose innocent victims are legion... We have in this century seen the growth of ideologies which have reduced their opponents to sub-human status or have subjected the poor and the powerless to deprivation and exploitation...

Are there then no signs of hope? Is there nothing to encourage and sustain us? I believe that God's grace is inexhaustible, his life a spring which never fails. There is a yearning for peace; more and more realize that war is never the way to resolve conflict. There are signs that people are no longer prepared to tolerate injustice and deprivation for others.

Basil Hume

Desert Soil

I've shut the door,
bombast and debate stilled to silence.
Sand clouds from the challenging tanks subside
into the Wilderness of Presence.
No bush bursts into flame,
but, instant as a heart beat, sounds the human cry
"Sir, come down,
come down before my child dies".

Once it was a father, pleading for a son in Capernaum.
Now the intercession serves the mother
whose boy smiled at the camera,
on mannequin parade with his platoon,
displaying the gear
designed to thwart the gas and germs
of a mad scientist's war.
It's spoken in Iraqi, Kurdish, Arabic
and all the Babel tongues that sound
across the lands of Abraham's Sons.

"... before my child dies".
The hunger-gaunt faces
and match-stick arms
make another plea
from the parched earth of Africa,

as climate, debt or political corruption
dry the dust of death.

The desert's holocaust
is summoned by human choice.
Oil-rich consumers and their armaments
have robbed the poor.
Only the small change of charity
funds the famine appeals
because the wealth of nations
is spilt in the sand
of economic empire.

"Come down...".
No clouds will part to save us.
The divine response of healing
is not a thunderclap of might
but the soft rain of human tears.
Then we must make the choice
which either lets them run into the ground
or feed a watered garden.
Only beware, the time is short
before God's children die
and take our future with them.

Michael Hare Duke

Refusing to Hate

I was at Al-Aqsa mosque that day. I was a witness to
everything. I never witnessed so much hatred, bitterness
and thirst for blood as I did that day. Border guards
were aiming their guns to kill. Demonstrators were
running for their lives. It was a tragic disaster.

It was as if a mirror was placed in front of me and I

could see what was happening behind me. I could see blood dripping from my back. I could sense fear and doubt. Soldiers had arrested me by then and I was ordered to stand by a wall. They were insulting me and I was trying with all my strength to defend my dignity.

They said, "Bend your head". I said, "You can smash my head but you can never make me submit." I wondered then if I were truly alive, if that bullet aimed at my head did not actually hit me. Did I die and was now reborn? The place was filled with feelings of hatred, bitterness, doubt and the desire for revenge. It was like a tornado had struck. The air was too heavy to breathe, especially after the police had fired tear-gas canisters in that holy site.

I could see the policemen dragging arrested people chained with plastic handcuffs, then beating them. One sadistic policeman seemed to enjoy pulling the men by the handcuffs and watching their pain as the blood almost stopped flowing to their hands. Were these hours of pain and waiting for an unknown event, or was this the pain of labour which will end in the birth of a new life?

No, that man who had occupied this body for years did not die but was born again with a stronger will and a deeper faith. I could see things more clearly. A special light was guiding my way.

The suffocating smell of tear gas, blood and gunfire filled the holy place. The sky was filled with clouds of death. I began to pray:

Lord, my breast is heavy with bitterness, let me not hate.
Lord, my heart is filled with pain, let me not avenge myself.
Lord, my soul is fearful, let not that fear turn into hatred.

Lord, my body is weak, let me not despair.

Lord, I am one of your worshippers standing at a crossroads, sustain my strength.

Lord, to believe is to love, to forgive and never to doubt. Faith is a light that guides the way, put not that light out.

Lord, protect our unarmed uprising and grant us the strength not to strike back at those who hurt us.

Lord, we only want to win our freedom and not to enslave others.

Lord, we want a state that will be a home to which our dispersed people can return. We do not seek to destroy the states or homes of other people.

Lord, we have nothing, except our faith in You. Give us the feeling of certainty, the will to stay.

Lord, let forgiveness and mercy prevail amongst us and let the blood that spilled from our bodies make us stronger and more steadfast against hatred and revenge.

Lord, hear my prayers and show me and my people the true path.

Faisal Husseini

A Peacemaking Church

The fundamental challenge for humanity today – and this is especially true for the disciple of Jesus – is to make peace – even in the midst of war.

Our vocation – now more than ever – demands that we be a peacemaking Church – a church of activists

– constantly praying for peace
– constantly acting for peace

100

– and therefore constantly reflecting peace
– reflecting peace in our attitudes, our ambitions, our relationships, our inter-action with all those who serve us in public office.

But a person – a community – a church – which speaks and acts for peace will also be acting for justice.
   Therefore, we will find ourselves consistently raising fundamental moral questions about the policies of governments

– about the sale of arms
– about what motivates particular policies
– about the effects such policies have on others, not least the hungry and the poor of the world.

A peacemaking Church is a community which excludes nobody, especially those most in need.
   Tonight, those most in need include those who are engaged in war, and those who are casualties of war – on all sides of the conflict.
   We pray particularly for those whom we know and love who are serving with the armed Forces.
   And we pray for their families who are most directly touched by the fear which war brings.
   We pray too for the leaders of all nations, not least those engaged in this war

– we pray that they may act upon the words of Pope
   Paul VI:
                    "War never again! Never again!"

Thomas Winning

The Way of Forgiveness

When the story is told
of enemy atrocities
and our own abuses of human rights

how shall we forgive?
how shall we learn to live?

In the aftermath of war
in the exaltation of success
and the bitterness of defeat

how shall we forgive?
how shall we learn to live?

When lives are spent,
cities derelict, the land destroyed
and the cost is reckoned

how shall we forgive?
how shall we learn to live?

When we are confronted with terror
and evil done in the name of justice;
when we are torn by anger and shame

how shall we forgive?
how shall we learn to live?

Take us to the Cross
– that God-forsaken place
of violence and brutality –

.and we shall find our forgiveness
and learn the way to life.

Jan Berry

Making the Connection

Just before Christmas I received a letter from a friend
in Dongora, a rural area in Southern Ethiopia. She
wrote about the famine and poverty which has brought
so much misery and suffering to the people of that
region. It was painful to read, especially because I was
there on a visit a few years ago and I'd come to know
some of those people.

This week, "The Crisis in Africa Appeal" alerted us to
the fact that as many as twenty million people in
different parts of Africa are suffering in the same way.
The aid agencies warn that unless we act now, many of
these people will fact a slow and silent death. When
famine struck Ethiopia in 1984, a big question for many
was "Why does God allow it?" It was as if dealing with
this tragedy was completely beyond our human
capabilities, and we needed to blame God for failing to
respond in time. But the massive response to the Gulf
crisis proves that the rich nations are quite capable of
finding both the money and the personnel to deal with
an emergency when it suits them. The question then
about what's happening in Africa is not "Why does God
allow it?" but "Why do *we* allow it?"

People justify the response to the Gulf on the grounds
that the whole credibility of the United Nations rests
on its ability to take decisive action in support of Kuwait.
But this line of argument seems to overlook the fact
that the United Nations itself was founded on the belief
that every human being has the right to life, liberty

and security. For the twenty million people in Africa now facing starvation these rights are no more than words on paper. The credibility of the United Nations then demands much more than just being able to act together over Kuwait. Twenty years ago Pope Paul VI called on the world to take decisive action in order to solve once and for all the problems of hunger and war. He described the situation of the poor in many parts of our world as unjust and evil. He reminded the rich nations that they in particular had a responsibility to use their wealth for the good of all. Pope Paul offered us a vision of the world where all people could fulfil their full human potential. The Gospel, he believed, demanded nothing less. But in his vision the people of Africa are as important as the people of the Middle East.

In other words, we can't claim to be our neighbours' keeper in one part of the world and at the same time ignore the plight of millions elsewhere.

Oliver McTernan

8

Nurturing

Being Human

Being human pushes us towards being daring, to taking risks, to overreaching ourselves, to being the lone hero, to being stupendously strong, to being in control, powerful, to showing others, to fierce ecstasy, either of anger or of sexual conquest. Useless to pretend that we are not like that, that power and destruction are not exciting for us, and part of our vitality.

Being human inclines us to nurturing and protecting, to loving and protecting what is frail – a baby or a kitten – to feeding and nourishing, to offering comfort and support and wisdom, to the long patience of gestating the embryo in the womb, and the longer patience of nursing it in infancy. It inclines us to care for the earth itself and all its creatures. It likewise inclines us to the gestating of words or ideas or symbols or sounds, in order to trace the pattern of which we are a part. It makes poets and painters, composers and playwrights, doctors and mothers.

This is our double inheritance, but the first half of it, which may have been crucial to human survival, now has to yield supremacy to the second inheritance, or there will be no babies, no kittens, no poets, no earth – just devastation. This is the big change, the Great

Task, as the Eskimos say, upon which everything depends.

Monica Furlong

The Mirage of Dr Abdin

We sat on the carpet, the Professor of Chemical Pathology at Cairo University and I – then a BBC interviewer trying to make a film about Islam. He had picked the location: his private mosque tucked at the back of his house where the garage might be. It was a late-night interview, preceded by hours of chanting, from which we were excluded; though we arrived in time to stand in the starry dark outside and hear the concluding exhalations, the Names of God ecstatically repeated like a great, winding, male, vocal rosary. The professor's cronies (among them, a banker, a teacher, a civil engineer, a publisher) emerged and scattered into the night. We were invited in.

Between him and me there was a small lectern. We both sat on equal cushions. The room was unadorned, except for the *mihrab*, the arrow-head niche that establishes the direction of Mecca. A curtain separated a modest corner of the room from the part we were in. Behind it, the professor's wife settled down respectfully to overhear the interview.

It was a question about Hell that produced the first long sigh from behind the curtain. The professor had answered two or three questions already, now and then glancing to the curtain with what I took to be a husband's solicitude. But something he said about Hell did not please his wife and she let him know. He asked to rephrase his answer. From the curtain there was silence. But not for long. The first interruptions were a few whispered words, leading to a more comprehensive discussion of each question he was asked and each answer he offered. Eventually, she ducked under the curtain into the main mosque and – since we were not at prayer and no public were present – slid along the carpet to join us. From then on, though her husband articulated the answers, they jointly examined the questions before he spoke. He was not hen-pecked. He was hen-affirmed, and his feathers were not (as far as I could see) ruffled.

The next time I saw the professor's wife was years later, quite by chance, in Regent Street in London. She was walking past the glitzy windows, a diminutive figure in a plain, long, brown coat and tight headscarf, carrying her one piece of hand luggage. "Dr Abdin?" I ventured, half expecting the mirage to fade. "What are you doing here?" "I'm on my way to Leeds", she answered. "The University is giving me an honorary doctorate tomorrow and I have just two hours to be a tourist before the train leaves from King's Cross."

So someone in Leeds knew about Dr Abdin's solo initiative in founding a children's hospital for rheumatic heart diseases near the pyramids of Gizeh. They acknowledged her pioneering medical research. They saluted an indomitable, humane campaigner for funds, resources and attention in a field that, until her arrival, Egyptian medicine had undervalued.

As we parted and, slight, sombre, eyes down, she threaded her way through the Regent Street shoppers, I found myself wondering if anyone would notice her; and, if they did, what they would make of her. She could so easily be mistaken for just another example of oppressed, unadorned, colourless, Islamic womanhood, paroled for a morning's shopping from her master's kitchen.

It would not be so bad if the mirage of Dr Abdin were

the only issue on which we mis-gauge and belittle Islam.
But she is just one grain of sand in a mighty desert.

Ronald Eyre

Hard Weather

My resident robin
demonstrates his rage,
and with good reason.
His private patch has been polluted
by last year's fledglings,
anxious for a perchhold
in the lengthening crumb dole.
And, as they scarcely seem to bother
to remove their small fluffed bodies
from my well-worn trackway
between back door and bird feast,
I reason with these creatures
who have so nearly taken me on trust
With my benevolent dispensing of supplies
"Why do you spend your precious energy
in tempestuous tribal warfare?
Why can't you share the little that there is
so all might then survive?"
I ask in vain. The robin chirps his irritation,
and I depart, defeated, for more stale breadcrumbs.
And wonder why I am trying to save these diminutive
    heart beats,
When children are due for dying in the deserts?

Baa Hare Duke

Dining in Heaven or Hell

There was a rabbi who wanted to see both Heaven and Hell. And God, who has hidden from us the opposites and their unity, gave way to his pleading.

The rabbi found himself before a door, which bore no name, he trembled as he saw it open before him. It gave into a room, and all was prepared for a feast. There was a table, and at its centre a great dish of steaming food. The smell and the aroma inflamed the appetite. The diners sat around the table with great spoons in their hands, yet they were shrieking with hunger, and fainting with thirst in that terrible place. They tried to feed themselves, and gave up, cursing God, the author and origin of their torment. For the spoons God had provided were so long that they could not reach their faces and get the food to their tongues. They stretched out their arms, but their mouths remained empty. So they starved because of these spoons while the dish of plenty lay amongst them. And the rabbi knew their shriekings were the cries of Hell. And as knowledge came, the door closed before him.

He shut his eyes in prayer, and begged God to take him away from that terrible place. When he opened them again, he despaired, for the same door stood before him, the door that bore no name. Again it opened, and it gave onto the same room. Nothing had changed, and he was about to cry in horror. There was the table, and at its centre the steaming bowl, and around it were the same people, and in their hands the same spoons.

Yet the shrieking had gone, and the cries and the curses had changed to blessings. And nothing had changed, yet everything. For with the same long spoons they reached to each other's faces, and fed each other's mouths. And they gave thanks to God the author and origin of their joy.

And as the rabbi heard the blessings, the door closed.
He bent down, and he too blessed God who had shown
him the nature of Heaven and Hell, and the chasm – a
hairsbreadth wide – that divides them.

Lionel Blue

Mother of Tears

O woman, wherefore art thou come
to Baghdad town on a winter's day?
I come to look for my only son,
for the soldiers came and took him away.

What is his name, O mother of tears,
what is the name of your only son?
His name is Peace, he is young and shy,
and the soldiers came and took him away.

He has gone to the war, O mother of tears,
he has gone to the front with the older men.
He rides on a tank with his head held high,
His cheeks afire in the evening light.

When will he come home, my only son?
When will the war be over, sir?
When will he come home to his weeping bride,
return to his father and sisters and me?

How can I know, O mother of tears,
How can we know the minds of men
who sit afar off and make their plans
out of sight of the sand, the blood and the tears.

They are the people who make this war,
to us it is given to weep and wait,
not knowing the rights and wrongs of it all –
knowing only the sound of death in the night.

Lord our God, we pray for mothers of soldiers
everywhere, for all the women of the Middle East,
whose tears run as freely as our own. Please comfort us
and bring this terrible war to an end.

Sheila Cassidy

The Reminder

The king held a great feast for his craftsmen – artificers,
smiths and armourers.

They came with gifts and they presented them after
the banquet: jewelled swords, matched daggers, shields
studded with silver.

One man – the last in line – had nothing. He stood up
and recited a poem about blue skies and woolly clouds.

The king smiled.

All present took that as a mark of his disdain. They
began to chuckle, catcall, jeer. Their derision mounted
in volume.

The king stood up. "Why do you laugh at my poem?"
he asked.

The silence was like a slammed door.

"My father", said the king, "sent me, when I was a
boy, to lodge with this man and his family so that I
could find out at first hand how my people live. I made
poems. I told them to my host." The king bowed to the
old man. "He has remembered. Today he has given me

a priceless gift. You brought me things that remind me of who I am. He brought me something that reminds me of who I used to be."

David Ogston

The Secret Dancers

When we were little, they said, "Do not climb up that tree; it is too high, too dangerous." It was a tree that soared above the house, the barn, the long byre.

The day came when we fell out with one another, my cousin and I. We traded insults, and even lumps of hair. She went off alone. And I was left to ponder some act of assertion.

The tree. I climbed the tree, my feet waltzing on its upper limbs, my heart fluttering with fear. At last I was so high that I could look down into the broken skylight of the loft.

And there she was. All alone in the bare loft, oblivious of everything, unaware of me upon my taboo territory. And she was dancing – pirouettes, and arabesques, and flourishes. My lumpish cousin.

I watched her for a long time. Then she looked up and saw me. At once we knew we had an equal power – the power to hurt each other.

But to this day, we neither of us have betrayed that moment, the moment when we danced together and rose above the things that limit us.

David Ogston

Women and Things

Women make things grow:
Sometimes like the crocus,
surprised by rain, emerging fully
grown from the belly of the earth;
Others like the palm tree with
its promise postponed,
rising in a slow
deliberate
spiral to the sky.

Women make things light
afloat
like the breathless
flight of soap bubbles
shimmering in the eyes of a lone
child in a forbidden schoolyard;
And heavy
like the scent of an over-ripe fruit
exploding at the
knowledge of summer-hardened
soil on days of siege.

Women make things smooth
to the touch,
like the kneading of
leavened bread at the dawn of hunger;
And coarse
like the brush of a
home-spun coat on
care-worn shoulders and bare
arms barely touching on the night of deportation.

Women make things cold
sharp and hard
like a legal argument thrust
before the threat of search and detention;
Or warm
and gentle like
justice in a poem,
like the suggestion of
the image of freedom
as a warm bath and
a long soak, in an undemolished home.

Women make things –

And as we, in separate
worlds, braid
our daughters' hair
in the morning, you and
I, each
humming to herself, suddenly
stops
and hears the
tune of the other.

Hanan Mikhail-Ashrawi

9

Prayer for the Enemy

Christian Prayer for our Enemies

Most merciful and loving Father,
We beseech Thee most humbly, even with all our
    hearts,
To pour out upon our enemies with bountiful hands
    whatsoever things Thou knowest may do them good.
And chiefly a sound and uncorrupt mind,
Where-through they may know Thee and love Thee in
    true charity and with their whole heart,
And love us, Thy children, for Thy sake.
Let not their first hating of us turn to their harm,
Seeing that we cannot do them good for want of
    ability.
Lord, we desire their amendment and our own.
Separate them not from us by punishing them,
But join and knot them to us by Thy favourable
    dealings with them.
And, seeing we be all ordained to be citizens of the one
    everlasting city,
Let us begin to enter into that way here already by
    mutual love,
Which may bring us right forth thither.

Elizabethan Prayer Book

Ishmael, My Brother

Ishmael, my brother,
How long shall we fight each other?

My brother from times bygone,
My brother – Hagar's son,
My brother, the wandering one.

One angel was sent to us both,
One angel watched over our growth –
There in the wilderness, death threatening
through thirst,
I a sacrifice on the altar, Sarah's first.

Ishmael, my brother, hear my plea:
It was the angel who tied thee to me...
Time is running out, put hatred to sleep.
Shoulder to shoulder, let's water our sheep.

Shin Shalom

Seeing a Face

Demanding God,
who reverses all my expectations
and challenges every prejudice,
confront me with Christ's radical precept
that I "love my enemy".
Cut away the spiralling violence
of ideas and invective
in which "our side" clothes my enemy,
and by which he becomes a mere object.
Let me see his face.
And then, let me not smash the mirror

you have given me to contemplate,
but may I breathe a greeting to one
who feels and bleeds as I do.
And may I embrace
the dark shadow within
instead of disowning it
and laying it upon another –
whom I call my enemy
but whom you destined to be
my neighbour and my friend.

Kate Compston

"Love Your Enemies"

What do we do with Jesus' command to love our enemies
in a time of war? What could once be seen as a bland
statement suddenly takes on a new and challenging
sharpness. Do we see it as easy appeasement – a passive
acceptance of injustice? Or impractical politics – a nice
ideal in personal relationships, but with nothing to say
to us politically?

Yet Jesus spoke in the highly-charged political
situation of occupied territory – ruled by a regime that
could abuse human rights and put down rebellion and
revolt as brutally as anything we might imagine in
Iraq, El Salvador, South Africa or Northern Ireland.
Along with others, Jesus was eventually killed by that
regime as a political subversive.

Underlying the teaching of Jesus about love for
enemies is His understanding of God as the father of
all.

The idea of God as father can be used too glibly and
cosily in terms of a personal and private relationship to
God (although it is true that Jesus sometimes uses it to

suggest intimacy). It has been (justifiably) criticised by feminists when it is used to suggest a male patriarchal image of God to the exclusion of all others. Its radicalness, however, lies in its inclusiveness. If God is father of us all, then we are all God's children. If we all have one parent, then we are all brothers and sisters.

So Jesus, talking to the Jews, was telling them that the hated Romans were their brothers and sisters.

The writers of the gospels, recording His words, were saying to the fragile, potentially-divided communities of Jews and Gentiles, rich and poor, slaves and free, women and men, that "they", the others who were despised or feared, were their brothers and sisters.

To us, these words are saying that Saddam Hussein and the Iraqi people whose cities were our targets – these are our brothers and sisters.

This is the radical challenge to our thinking and our praying – to refuse to see "the enemy" as wholly other, alien, a different species who can be dehumanized and so destroyed without compunction, but as human beings like ourselves, our brothers and sisters.

Whatever we believe about the rights and wrongs of the conflict, this is how we must pray; not only for our own friends and relatives and their safety, not with any conviction of a God who cares only for our welfare, but for all our brothers and sisters. For how else can we pray with Jesus "Our Father…"?

Jan Berry

A Prayer for Saddam Hussein and George Bush

O God, you fill the universe
with light and love.

In you we live and move
and have our being.
We pray for Saddam Hussein
and George Bush.
Enlighten their minds
and fill their hearts
with the power of your creative love.
Guide their actions
so that all civilians
and soldiers in the Gulf area
are protected
from the sufferings of war.
Inspire their decisions
so that the crisis in the Middle East
is resolved peacefully,
and all peoples of the world
learn to walk in ways of justice,
love and peace.
Amen

Pax Christi, USA

Enemy

This meditation continues the process of learning to
deal with everyday situations. We are trying to find out
why we think, say and do so many unnecessary, or
even harmful things. In the last part of this process we
came to see that since the qualities of Buddha are in all
beings, then size is of no importance. It becomes possible
to increase and decrease the size of the body, as well as
change its shape. Thus we begin to realize how we
might free ourselves from its limitations.

The object of the present exercise is to confront
aversion. Even if you don't have an enemy whom you

intensely dislike, it is still possible to do this exercise because there are different categories of enemy and different degrees of enmity:

a) Enmity based on one's own aversion: this can range in intensity from the slight, where someone frequently annoys or irritates you, to the extreme, where there is a great feeling of anger and hatred which could even make you want to kill.

b) Enmity based on another's aversion: which is where another person sees all you do in negative terms.

c) Enmity based on clinging: which describes a situation where you become very intensely attached to another person. In this instance, the mind always goes to that person and one is constantly preoccupied with her or him. This form of attachment might have the appearance, or label, of "love", but it actually enslaves the mind and results in suffering.

The Exercise

In this particular meditation exercise we will focus on the form and feelings of the enemy rather than the speech or activity. Begin the session by selecting a particular person who falls into one of the above categories of enmity, no matter how strong or weak the enmity may be.

Imagine that person sitting in front of you. With most of your in-breaths (not all), bring the enemy into you. Take in all of his or her feelings, sensations, thoughts, fears, inner organs and so on. With most of your out-breaths, let all of your feelings, etc., flow out of you into the enemy.

This process continues until your "qualities and attributes" and those of your enemy are fully exchanged, leaving the outer forms unchanged.

After the exchanging is complete, begin to reflect:

Where is the anger? Where's the hatred, the fear, the imprisoning attachment? Where is the cause of enmity? Think to yourself: "Now that I am the enemy and the enemy is me, where is the source of the feeling?"

Having completed the exchanging and reflection, come back to your own form and feelings, but keep the understanding of the other. Move on to the relaxing meditation – simply allowing thoughts and feelings to flow freely. Let the mind relax and observe whatever comes and goes.

This exercise goes to the heart of our problems. It may at times be very painful, but be courageous and carry on.

Do this exercise once a day for about an hour and twenty minutes, leaving ten minutes at the end for relaxation. It is best to keep the focus on a few people, not changing too often. Continue the meditation for four weeks.

Question: *Although I understand that this exercise is designed to change my own mind rather than the mind of anyone else, I can't help thinking that, since I'm working so hard on myself, there ought to be some improvement in the other. Is this the wrong way to look at it?*

Rinpoche: Fundamentally the idea is not to bring about change in anyone else. Whilst there may be some improvement in others, the aim and result should be positive change in oneself.

Question: *You suggest that the state of being in love could be considered as a kind of enmity. Does this mean we should run away when we feel strongly attracted to another person, or is it possible to purify the love at the heart of the attraction so that it becomes useful?*

121

Rinpoche: If you love without clinging, or if you can overcome any clinging which may initially arise, then that love will be very, very useful. However, whenever there is clinging to the object of love, or to the idea of love itself, then the love is tainted and easily spoiled. Since clinging leads to other negative tendencies, such as expectation, possessiveness and jealousy, wherever there is clinging the purity of love is lost.

Question: *While doing this exercise I've experienced the feeling of being taken over by someone whom I suspect of really wishing to harm me. This was so frightening that it was several days before I felt safe in myself again. Should I persist with the exercise in spite of this?*

Rinpoche: If you're practising this exercise in a completely pure and loving way, then the idea of someone taking over your life can be seen as a very welcome development rather than as something negative. But if you're only a beginner, unable to see it in this way, it would be helpful to try to improve your understanding of the Buddha within. So, should this fear arise again, try to develop awareness of the Buddha nature within yourself, and repeat the exercise.

Question: *Sometimes this exercise has a very disturbing effect on me – I get very upset and carried away by strong and bitter emotions. Is it better to carry on and try to go right through these experiences, or should I stop and practise relaxation?*

Rinpoche: Both approaches have their place. At the beginning, some relaxation may be helpful; but at some stage it will be necessary to face the situation, however difficult, and overcome it. In the end it's necessary to go right through and beyond it.

Akong Rinpoche

A Prayer for the Chiefs of Command

"You love all that exists. You hold nothing of what you have made in abhorrence, for had you hated anything, you would not have formed it."

Take a photograph of Saddam Hussein from the newspaper. Look at it carefully, memorizing the features. Now close your eyes and imagine that you are in an underground bunker deep in Iraq. Look around the walls at the charts and maps. Observe the objects and the equipment in the room; try to capture some of the atmosphere.

Now look at the face of the man. What are the conflicting emotions and desires expressed in that face? Name them without judging them.

Now bring God into the picture. You may be able to imagine the figure of Jesus in that bunker.

Formulate a prayer for Saddam Hussein in that situation and speak it out loud... Now express your own emotions and desires, asking for healing and reconciliation.

Allow the picture to fade and spend a little time returning to your own room.

Repeat the whole exercise with a photograph of George Bush in his private office in the White House.

Hilary Elliott

10

Summing it all Up

Our Father in the Desert

The Lord's Prayer sets a pattern for all praying. One
way of using it is to pause over every phrase to allow its
full meaning to sink in. Here's what can happen as the
well-known words kindle one's imagination.

Since the Gulf was my concern the desert seemed a
natural place to be, the sand, hazardous not with
scorpions but land-mines, stretching to the horizon.
The words begin:

Our The place is solitary but I am not alone. Like a
sound wave in the ether my prayer ripples out. The
phrases echo in the hearts of friends and then spread
worldwide in every language. The issues humming in
my head feel overwhelming but they are matched by
the energy of all the people with whose prayer my
solitude is joined.

Beyond the contemporary world are those who have
experienced the wars and disasters, the delights and
the horrors of other generations. Prayer brings together
the great democracy of the dead. We all gather in the
presence of our Father.

Being human we narrow our company to the like-
minded. The God to whom we pray knows no limitations.

125

Every child is His. When our blinkered vision lets us sing a Te Deum to celebrate our victory, He weeps for the hurt of those we have conquered. When all belong together "Our" means everyone.

Father We are talking not to a King or a Commander, not to a superior or a controller. We communicate within a relationship of love. Parents by nature want to see their children develop their own individual gifts and grow free. It costs a lot to allow them to make mistakes and accept the heartache of watching things go wrong. God too comes as the vulnerable self-denying parent, not as a colonial administrator, cosmic nanny, or ultimate insurance. We choose and He lets us have our way.

He trusts me with my life. Do I trust others – or do I want to tell them what is best?

In heaven Is He cheating after all, floating safely above the world and its distress? Pious fantasy has painted a golden city, idle and secure. Jesus embodies the exchange that links heaven and earth. As the image of His return to heaven is unfolded He promises "I am with you always to the end of time". Heaven is our experience transfigured by the wisdom and the healing of the Father.

As I stand in the desert, battered by the fear and anger of the battle and loosely call it Hell, the Father's compassion for His children hovers above it, absorbing all the prayers and all the cries, to weave them into the basic notes from which hope can find a song. Heaven is not another place, it is the wilderness that has become a watered garden.

Your name be hallowed Mostly I want the glory, reputation, even the call of love to be for me. Competition, rivalry, enmity colour my motives; "noted by my name". This conflict is all about power, possessions and prestige.

Your "name" takes that away. You are the servant, the crucified. You meet us in the poor, the non-celebrities, the weak. You are there when the tank commander weeps for the men who have died, in the frailty of the pilot who flies in spite of all his fears. You are there in the civilian casualties and in the frightened child who lurks in the heart of the tyrant. You are in the vulnerable bit of me that is scared to say such things.

Help me to acknowledge that and know that when I make the grand gesture or posture for applause, You are denied. Here in the desert let Your name be hallowed, in acts of generosity and force.

Your kingdom come It's power again. A human kingdom needs defending. Security requires frontiers, and armour to defend them. The boundaries of Kuwait have become the cause, excuse, for war. Millions of dollars, that the world can ill afford, are squandered on weapons while famine forces the poor to scratch an instant crop from soil no longer fertile and to burn the trees whose continuance would nourish the land.

In Your kingdom the hungry are fed and the inheritors are the poor. What we defend, we lose; what we let go, becomes inalienably ours. The kingdom comes as gift, not conquest. The condition is only that we want it.

Your will be done, on earth as in heaven If only we knew what it was! We try to obey and find we've got it wrong. What seemed so good turns out for the worst. There is no easy guide; today's love, viewed with tomorrow's hindsight, appears like manipulation.

The clue lies in the way we make our choices, not in choosing one course rather than another. When I get

127

rigid and defensive, I fight my corner, trapped in the armour of my will. Your obedience sets me free. I can repent and start again to seek for what You want.

Then I hear Your gentle laughter which forgives the frantic children, salving their bruised pride by breaking heads or hearts.

Give us today our daily bread The emphasis is again on gift; my hands held open not clenched for fight. Receiving and giving construct the circle of generosity. Adversaries face each other in lines of confrontation. Our anxiety to get all we can, has denied partnership. We dominate the earth and one another, only secure when we can make others afraid.

Once the stranger in the desert could count on hospitality, because even an alien was a brother with a claim on a shared meal. Now in a hungry world we guard our foodstocks for ourselves, sell the surplus to the highest bidder. Today's bread was sold last year in a future's market.

Forgive us our sins All the mistakes that brought us to this place make up a long account of accusation: pursuit of my advantage blinded me to wider worries, cowardice clamped my tongue from speaking unpopular warnings, I ignored others and devalued those who might have made up my deficiencies.

Some guilt we share: corporate greed that profited by trading arms in an area of danger; the international blindness that denied justice to the landless because their complaint lacked muscle; the chosen deafness to the cries of tortured, persecuted people. Others reap death from the sins we've sown by our unwisdom, selfishness and silence.

Yet nurturing a cactus crop of guilt will heal nothing. Its prickly fruit will yield a sterile self-absorption. Set

128

us free for action so that the desert can flower with justice.

As we forgive those who sin against us To acknowledge my fault means I have no need to heap the blame on someone else. If there is a demon tyrant then I helped him grow. No one section of the human race, no individual is totally to be condemned. The Patriot in shining armour confronting the scummy Scud blocks the healing which the whole family must seek. Their beastliness sprang from the soil of my failure. My forgiveness is bound up with theirs.

If I use others to camouflage my responsibility, no forgiveness follows. The cheap anodyne device of loading all I've done onto the scapegoat's back proves that I have not understood why Jesus died.

Lead us not into temptation We've chosen the trial of strength, the test of nerve. So have they. Confident calculations have given way to a gambler's guess. "He'll never do it": "We're bound to win." We fell for the temptation to trust the strength of tanks, Tornados, Tomahawks.

But now we're testing men. The tense nerves waiting under the camouflage nets, fear of the unknown, and courage asked of others by those who made the choices. In human terms we've failed already.

Help us to meet the test of the humility which turns again. Christ's apostles were not flawless souls who never failed. They learned to ask for strength, to fear the trial unless God's power went with them. That's the honesty that makes real prayer.

Deliver us from evil I want to pray that horrors will never happen; that all I fear will go away. But You are not that kind of God. You let the Jews of old go into captivity because that was where their denial led them. It is no use asking to be saved from the consequences of our actions.

We need the help to cope with history so that we do not become vindictive, bitter, hard. What comes by way of suffering from outside hurts; but the evil that wells up within is what destroys. Christ of the wilderness, save us from the devils within ourselves.

Michael Hare Duke

PART II

11

A Quarry of Prayer

God of our Fathers,
great and merciful God,
Lord of peace and life,
Father of all.

You have plans of peace, and not of affliction.
You condemn wars
and defeat the pride of the violent.

You sent Your Son Jesus
to preach peace
to those who are near and far away,
to gather people of every race and nation
into a single family.

Hear the single-hearted cry of your children,
the anguished plea of all humanity:
no more war, an adventure without return,
no more war, a spiral of death and violence;
no war in the Persian Gulf,
a threat against all your creatures
in heaven, on the earth and in the sea.

In communion with Mary, the Mother of Jesus,
once again we implore you:

speak to the hearts of those responsible
for the fate of peoples,
stop the "logic" of revenge and retaliation;
with your Spirit suggest new solutions,
generous and honourable gestures,
room for dialogue and patient waiting which are
more fruitful than the hurried deadlines of war.

Give our era days of peace.
War no more. Amen.

Pope John Paul II

Almighty God, Creator of the Universe,
I feel very small and helpless
in the face of the atrocities of war between nations.
I offer you the only thing I can –
my ordinary, everyday life.
I ask you to take it into your hands
and to use it to bring peace.
I do not ask to understand
but only to accept that you need very little
in order to do much,
for you once fed five thousand hungry people
with five loaves and two fish,
the gift of one small boy.

Sister Frances Dominica

Almighty God, we are the family of humankind. Look
upon us in mercy. We are your children and all of us
have sinned. Help us to look at you: help us to look at
one another.

We are one with all people everywhere. Forgive us

134

the greed which creates or condones injustice. Forgive what we have done by lifestyle and by choice to make the world unstable and unsafe.

And now that there is war again on earth help us to be at peace with you. Forgive our sins and renew our faith. Come to all who suffer. Use us to bring your help to all who are touched by tragedy. Let your light shine on the causes of war, and let your love dwell on its casualties.

May those whose policies create the conflict see new light and find new ways. Guide the leaders of the armed Forces to decisions which will save lives and shorten the conflict.

Give to the peoples of the Middle East a vision of their life as you would have it be and help them share it with the world.

As we grieve for the wounds mankind inflicts upon itself we stand in awe of the wounds we inflict upon You, the bearer of our sins and sorrows. We are the body of Christ who hung upon the Cross. By His Cross and passion break the cycle of sin and death. By His resurrection bring new life and hope. We ask for His Spirit that we may pray in His name. Amen.

David Sheppard

Lord of peace, we ask you to bring your peace to the
    Gulf.
But it is not any peace we ask.
We don't want a false peace based on fear, repression
    or destruction.
Peace is not the silence of cemeteries, the product of
    terror and death.
Peace cannot come through hatred, violence, the use
    of arms.

Lord, your peace is based on justice and love.
We ask that justice may be done in the Gulf.
We pray for the people of Kuwait that their country
   may be returned to them,
That they may be able to live there in freedom and
   peace.
We also pray for the Palestinian people that a just
   settlement may be reached between them and the
   Israelis.
We pray for justice for the Kurdish people and for
   other persecuted minority groups in the region.
We pray for the peoples of Iraq, Iran and all the Gulf
   States, that they may enjoy just democratic regimes
   where individual rights and freedoms are respected.

Lord, may we in the West, especially in this country,
   do all in our power to help build a just peace.
May we insist on the right conduct of a war we did not
   want.
May we refuse the use not only of nuclear or chemical
   weapons, but also of those conventional ones that
   are indiscriminate in their powers of destruction.
May we be firm in the resolution to avoid killing
   innocent civilians, to respect non-military
   installations, never to act out of revenge.
May we strengthen our determination to press for a
   cease-fire at the first possible opportunity, the first
   glimmer of hope for a just settlement.

Lord, we beg your pardon and forgiveness for the
   greed and selfishness that have caused this war.
Pardon for the aggressors and those who have
   connived with them.
Pardon also for some of those who have been attacked,
   albeit unjustly.
Especially we ask pardon for our own greed and

selfishness that have contributed to this war:

    for selling arms to the combatants,
    for coveting oil,
    for striving to maintain our high living standards
        at the expense of others.

Lord we ask your comfort and strength:

    for the courageous men and women fighting on both
        sides,
    for all who are suffering pain or bereavement,
    for divided families and refugees,
    for all those who are bewildered, anxious, afraid.

We pray for the Iraqi leaders, especially Saddam
    Hussein, that your gentleness and love may flow
    into their hearts.
We pray for our own leaders that they may be
    merciful, forgiving, far-sighted.
We pray finally for ourselves that we may learn to
    love our enemies as Christ taught us. Amen.

Michael Campbell Johnston SJ

Dear Lord,
    Our Holy land has become a land of holy terror.
Faith is turning sour, belief is turning to divisive dogma.
Conviction is turning to fanaticism. Care is turning to
fear, concern to frigidity, love is turning to greed. This
Holy land is not as Holy as it used to be.
    Dear Lord, teach us to build temples again. We have
turned temples into castles, we have made altars into
walls which divide. Our icons are no more as bright as
they used to be. Our candles are melting. The scent of
our incense is fading away.

137

Teach us to build temples from the sand and stones of ideas and aspiration. Help us sing the songs of peace and the hymns of justice.

Dear Lord, we may have exhausted Your patience with our sophisticated and decorated theology, with our elaborate ecclesiology, with our organization, with our institutionalism, with our statistics, with our desire to order the world to make it more secure. The final product is more insecurity. We speak of one God and act as if there are many. We talk of a living God and we treat Him as a statue when we refuse to see Him in every human being, in every nation, in every living faith, in every culture and in every phase of history.

In humility and love we stand to receive Your word. Come visit us. Let the Spirit turn our piety into authenticity. Let meaning transpire from our words.

In the name of Jesus Christ, our Lord, we pray.

Ghassan Rubeiz

O Lord soften the stone hearts
of those who preach and practise
intolerance and bigotry;
as the sun's setting glow
softens the stone walls
of Your Holy City, Jerusalem.

Lord, the rocky hills, the valleys
the deserts and the sea shores
are filled with the echoes of
centuries of pain.

Lord, bring peace to house and village.
Comfort the mothers who fret
and those who mourn.

Lord, keep strong the twisted old root
of the olive tree,
and protect the young vine.

Lord of water and stone,
of bread and wine,
Lord of resurrection,
feed hope, and bring peace
to this wracked but beautiful holy land.

Gerald Butt

So Abraham said: My Lord, make this city one of peace
and secure, and keep me and my sons from worshipping
idols. My Lord, they have led so many people astray!
Anyone who follows me belongs to me, while anyone
who disobeys me will still find You are forgiving,
merciful.

Our Lord, I have some of my offspring settle in a
valley without any crops, beside Your Hallowed House,
our Lord, so that they may keep up prayer. Make men's
hearts fond of them, and provide them with fruit that
they may be grateful.

Our Lord, You know whatever we hide and whatever
we display; nothing on earth nor in the sky is hidden
from God. Praise be to God Who has bestowed Ishmael
and Isaac on me in my old age. Surely my Lord hears
every appeal.

Praise be to God, Lord of the Universe,
the Merciful, the Mercy-Giving!
Ruler of the Day for Repayment!
You do we worship and from You do we seek help.
Guide us along the Straight Path,
the Road of those whom You have favoured,

with whom you are not angry, nor who are lost. Amen.

Contributed by Dr Mashuq Ally

O God, creator and sustainer of all things, Lord of infinite love, kindness and mercy, guide us to the way of love when hatred and pride appear to be the easier and more attractive way.

O God, cherisher and sustainer of all beings, sovereign Lord over all Your creation, in Your boundless mercy and care, teach us wisdom and compassion to face this threat of suffering, discord and death. Teach us, our most holy Creator, to love mercy and justice, as You love mercy and justice.

O God, Lord of all dominion in whose hands is all good, teach our leaders humility, wisdom and good judgement. Help us all to defuse this crisis peacefully before it plunges us into a whirlpool of senseless suffering, bloodshed and war.

O God, we give thanks to you for giving us this good earth as a sacred trust to enjoy and share with all your creatures. Help us to keep Your trust and not destroy it. Save us, our compassionate Lord, from our folly by Your wisdom, from our arrogance by Your forgiving love, from our greed by Your infinite bounty, and from our insecurity by Your healing power.

O God, guide us to Your ways, the ways of righteousness and peace. Grant us peace, O Lord of peace. Help us to do Your will in our lives, in our relations and in our affairs. Forgive us all, Your creatures, in Your mercy,

...d save us from our own evil.

Prayers for Peace in the Middle East – prepared by a Christian, a Jew and a Muslim

O Lord, we beseech You grant Your blessing and guidance to all who are seeking to bring peace to the Gulf area, the Middle East and the whole world; stir the conscience of the nations, and break the bonds of covetousness and pride; make plain Your way of deliverance, through Jesus Christ our Lord. Amen.

With All God's People

Sikh

Recognize all mankind, whether Hindu or Muslim, as
   one;
the same Lord is the Creator and Nourisher of all;
Recognize no distinction among them: the monastery
   and the mosque are the same;
So the Hindu worship and the Muslim prayer; men
   are all one.

Guru Gobind Singh

The One God is the Father of all
We are all his children;
O Guru, O Friend, I dedicate my heart to Thee,
If thou lettest me have but a glimpse of God.

Rag Sorath

141

Muslim

O God, You are peace. From You is peace and to You is peace. Let us live, O Lord, in peace and receive us in Your paradise, the abode of peace. Yours is the majesty and the praise, we hear and we obey. Grant us Your forgiveness, Lord, Lord, and to You be our becoming.

Prayer of the Prophet Muhammad (peace be upon him)

O Lord, Protect us from inhumanity and discrimination, hunger and poverty, death and starvation, violence and crime, hatred and prejudice, war and destruction, disgrace and humiliation, oppression and violation of human rights.

Let us, O Lord, witness faith and noble deeds, fraternity and kindness, far-sightedness and tolerance, forgiveness and piety, truth and justice, happiness and tranquillity, human dignity and unity, global peace and prosperity. Amen.

O Lord, let peace and justice prevail in the Middle East and the world at large. Amen.

Dr M I Surty (1989)

Hindu

O God, let us be united; let us speak in harmony; let
   our minds apprehend alike;
Common be our prayer, common the end of our
   assembly;
Common be our resolution; common be our
   deliberation.
Alike be our feelings; unified be our hearts;

142

Common be our intentions; perfect be our unity.

Rig Veda

I am a man of peace. But I do not want peace at any
price. I do not want the peace that you find in stone. I
do not want the peace that you find in the grave; but I
do want the peace which you find embedded in the
human breast, which is exposed to the arrows of the
whole world, but which is protected from all harm by
the power of Almighty God.

Mahatma Gandhi

In Prayer and Love
for one who has Died

The God of peace sanctify you completely,
even to the glory of the great day that is to come.
Faithful is the God who calls,
the God whose promises will be fulfilled.

N, God bless you richly,
grow in grace,
make love,
keep us in loving mind,
hold us close in the Presence,
guide us,
pray for us.

Jim Cotter

O God, Maker of all peoples,
save us from that loyalty to our country
which is blind unquestioning devotion;
and give us the harder loyalty
which challenges injustice
and insists on the claims of the Gospel. Amen.

O God
in whose light all that is covered will be revealed
and all that is hidden made known,
help us in our struggle to hold to the truth.

When accurate reporting is submerged
by government propaganda and journalistic bias,
help us in our struggle to hold to the truth.

When the language of technology and military
strategy
masks the realities of death and destruction,
help us in our struggle to hold to the truth.

When repetition gives the illusion of information
and we do not know what we are not being told,
help us in our struggle to hold to the truth.

O God of light
give us a passion for truth that will not be turned
aside
and a courage in declaring it that will not be silenced.
Amen.

ord Jesus Christ, in a world where people wander and constantly lose their tracks, You alone are the Way for us.

In a world of disloyalty and distrust, of broken promises and forgotten pledges, of compromise and deceit, You alone are the Truth for us.

In a world of casual cruelty and deliberate violence, of hatred and inhumanity, You alone are the Life for us.

You have given us a vision of a world that is Yours, and we call it Your Kingdom, where no sword is known but the sword of truth, and no strength is known but the strength of love. But in a world of violence, and threatened violence, of aggression, fear and anger, Your Kingdom seems a long way off. But to get there takes no time, and every moment can usher it in. Your Kingdom can be now.

So show us, good Lord,
How to be frugal till all are fed, and to be slaves till all are free,
how to weep till all can laugh, and to be meek till all can stand up in pride,
how to mourn till all are comforted, and to claim nothing till all find justice,
how to be restless till all live in peace, and to be hopeless ourselves, till all have hope.

Lord, in our doubting, speak to us of your certainty.
In our certainty, speak to us of your despair.
In our despair, speak to us of your hope.
In our hope, speak to us of your restlessness till all is peace.

We own our sorrow – and let it connect us with all those who suffer in this assault upon life. With the herders and farmers and townspeople now under our bombs. With the animals and birds of the desert, with the very stones of that ancient land, cradle of our civilization.

We own our shame – and let it reveal our connections with the weapons-makers and generals and politicians whose greed for profits and power led our people into this dark way.

We own our anger – and let it link us with all who are betrayed. All from whom the war-makers would divert our gaze. The hungry and homeless in our cities, and the children whose future we prepare.

We own our dread of what lies in store for us – and let it remind us of the fear that walks the streets of Baghdad and hides in the hearts of our warriors.

We own our weariness – and let it connect us with our ancestors, who tired, too, as they struggled forward through countless ordeals, in oppression and exile and long marches through the ages of ice. And so we connect with their endurance, too. They did not give up.

Though hard to bear, the sorrow and shame, the anger and fear and fatigue – each is a gift. For each can bring into focus our deep, invisible interconnections in the web of life. And lift us out of our narrow selves, and bring us into community across space and time. Each can open us to the boundless heart. Though found through pain, that boundless heart is real – and the ground of all healing.

Joanna Macy

146

r all those who came before us,
 or all those who gave from their hearts,
who gave from their lives,
that there might be a better world,
a safer world, a kinder world,
we pray for peace,
in their name.
That all their dreams,
that all their struggles,
would not end like this –
in this great sadness –
we pray for peace,
in their name.

And for the children,
that the children may live,
that they may have children of their own
and that it will go on –
this great blossoming that is meant
to go on and on –
we pray for peace,
in their name.
That they would have a world
worth being born into,
a future worth dreaming about,
that they might become, in their own time,
all that our race might come to be,
– that they might have that chance –
we pray for peace,
in their name.

And for the simple peoples of this earth,
who have no voice in this,
and for the animals
who have no voice in this,
and for the plants, the trees, the flowers,

147

who have no voice in this – for all those
who share this earth with us,
whose home this is, as much as our own –
we pray for peace,
in their name.

In this time, when we hold it all in our hands,
for all those who came before us,
for all those who would follow,
and for all those who share life with us
on this tiny, fragile, miraculous globe,
we pray that we – we who do have voices,
we who could speak out,
we who could take a stand,
we who could make a difference,
we pray that we may prove worthy
of this great, great trust
that we hold now in our care.

God the Father of all, deliver us from evil,
the evil of unjust governments and
tyrannical regimes, of religious
intolerance and racial strife, of war and
the loss of life;
deliver us from the evil
of world poverty in a world of abundant wealth.
Deliver us Lord from all evil;
and especially from the evil in ourselves;
let your kingdom come and your will be done,
for the glory of your name. Amen.

12

Tools for Worship

From peace that is no peace;
from the grip of all that is evil;
from a violent righteousness...   *deliver us.*

From paralysis of will;
from lies and misnaming;
from terror of truth...   *deliver us.*

From hardness of heart;
from trading in slaughter;
from the worship of death...   *deliver us.*

By the folly of Your Gospel;
by Your choosing our flesh;
by Your nakedness and pain...   *heal us.*

By Your weeping over the city;
by Your refusal of the sword;
by Your facing of horror...   *heal us.*

By Your bursting from the tomb;
by Your coming in judgement;
by Your longing for peace...   *heal us.*

Janet Morley

O God, compassionate and merciful,
where Your children tear each other
You also are torn.
Full of confusion, longing for peace,
we bring You our world,
threatened by violence
and enslaved by greed;
where the powerful can defend their interests
and the poor are trampled.
In this time of crisis,
open our hearts and minds to Your will,
and show us how to pray.

For those who have no power:

> trapped in hunger and the desert heat,
> workers from poor countries
> whose livelihoods are gone
> who wait in fear
> who face unemployment at home when they escape,

Lord in Your mercy – *hear our prayer*.

For those with power to help:

> struggling in makeshift camps
> to give shelter, food and care,
> and amid panic
> to organize relief;
> and for all who send support,

Lord in Your mercy – *hear our prayer*.

For all the nations affected:

> those strong enough to make their power felt,
> and those whose economies may be shattered;

those whose rich lifestyle is at risk,
and those who have not yet the basics of life;
those who resist invasion,
and those who still wait for a homeland;

Lord in Your mercy – *hear our prayer*.

May all who have the power to influence events
not be driven by arrogance,
but guided by Your justice.

Janet Morley

Lighting a Candle for Peace

This short service uses the action of lighting candles as
a way of focusing our prayers for peace. It can be
incorporated into any public act of worship, and was
used in St Ninian's Cathedral on Christmas night. It
can also be used by small groups or within a family.

With You, O Lord, is the well of life,
and in Your light we see light
With You, O Lord, is the well of life,
and in Your light we see light.

Your love, O Lord, reaches to the heavens,
and Your faithfulness to the clouds:
And in Your light we see light.

Glory to the Father, and to the Son and to the Holy
 Spirit.
With You, O Lord, is the well of life,
and in Your light we see light.

A candle is lit and put in a prominent place or in the centre of the group.

All say:

Rise up O Father, by Your power flowing:
   show to us vision, beauty and joy.
Rise up O Son, by Your cross bearing:
   show to us vision, beauty and joy.
Rise up O Spirit, by Your light glowing:
   show to us vision, beauty and joy.

Small candles may now be lit from the central candle.

Let us now bring God the gift of our prayer and of our silence.

> Father, as we ask for the grace to see You, we ask for the grace to see the world as You see it, to see both the joy and the sadness.
>   We turn our thoughts to the conflict in the Gulf, the peoples of that region, the powerful leaders of nations and the powerless little people, all those who carry arms and those who worry for their safety, all those who have died in the conflict and those who mourn them.

We offer this time of quiet and we burn these candles as signs of our desire for Your peace and Your justice to be experienced in the lives of all Your children.

During the silence may be sung the TAIZE chant
"Within our darkest night,
You kindle the fire that never dies away."

At the end of the silence:

God our Father, You gave us Your Son that we might share in Your life, the life which is light for all Your people: the light of hope, the light of justice, the light of compassion, the light of peace.

May these candles and the prayer they express shine in the dark places of our world and in the dark places of our hearts, and may Your Spirit bring us all clarity and healing. We ask this in the name of Jesus the Lord.

You, O Lord, are my lamp:
my God, You make my darkness bright.
You, O Lord, are my lamp:
my God, You make my darkness bright.

Kevin Franz

Light for the World

For some people prayer is helped by symbolic action. Three suggestions follow for an evening act of recollection. As darkness falls, light a candle saying the two prayers, the first from a Christian source, the second a Muslim.

The light of love burn in this flame,
consuming hatred,
purging the unforgiven past
promising a welcome to friend and stranger.

O God! Grant me light in my heart, light in my sight, light in my hearing, light to my left, light to my right, light above me, light beneath me, light before me, light behind me, and grant me light (*Prayers of the Prophet*).

When the candle is lit, place it in the window and say:

The Peace of God
shine from this place, reconciling division.

The Truth of God
light a path to trust between His children.

The Hope of God
roll back the darkness of despair.

Bread of Affliction

1. In church – in the context of the celebration of the Eucharist/Holy Communion/Lord's Supper.

Read Isaiah 30:15-26, then repeat and stress verse 20: "The Lord may give you bread of adversity and water of affliction, but He who teaches you shall no longer be hidden out of sight, but with your own eyes you shall see Him..." (NEB)

Use this verse to introduce a symbolic act in which – in sorrow and repentance – bread and water are brought forward and placed on a black cloth (on a small table in front of the white-clad Communion table). Appropriate sombre music may be played whilst the bread is rendered inedible with soil, and the wine undrinkable with vinegar – so that they represent "bread of adversity and water of affliction".

Then (in silence, or with a change to joyful music) move to the Communion table and uncover and/or raise the bread and wine. One way in which God becomes visible ("no longer hidden") for us, is in the bread/body and wine/blood of Christ, the incarnate Son.

Although present events call for our sorrow and repentance, God has not deserted us – and this we can celebrate even in and through our sadness. God is fulfilling the promise to bring us a feast very different from the "bread of adversity and the water of affliction": the eucharistic symbols of bread and wine are a foretaste of this feast in the Kingdom of shalom, as well as a recollection of Christ's complete self-giving for a broken world.

2. In church, in a small group, or with young people.
Read Genesis 9:1,6,9–15.

Talk briefly about water as an Hebraic symbol of chaos, disorder, distress – making links with the present "breakdown in peace and order".

Water in a large transparent bowl is brought forward and laid on a table.

Talk about the hope God promises, and recall the rainbow covenant.

Place seven or more variously coloured floating candles in the bowl of water, and invite different worshippers to light them. The principal participating nations in the Gulf War may be named and prayed for as each candle is lit.

Matthew 14:22-33 may also be read. And perhaps this poem:

Walking on water looks difficult,
but I have seen it done.

Those with enough grief to sink them
have kept on –
drawn by an invisible source

155

of strength
they were not let down.

Crossing this sea
some swim
and other drown,
but some there are
walking on water.

Cecily Taylor

Bring to mind and heart one of the cities affected by the
war, and pray as if you were a citizen living there now:

God, bless this city
and move our hearts with pity,
lest we grow hard.

God, bless this house
with courage, welcome, friendship,
and help us pray.

God, bless these days
of rough and narrow ways,
lest we despair.

God, bless the night
and calm the people's fright,
that we may love.

God, bless this land
and guide us with your hand,
lest we be unjust.

156

God, bless this earth
through pangs of death and birth,
and make us whole.

Jim Cotter

Contributors

Robert Runcie formerly Archbishop of Canterbury
Basil Hume Cardinal Archbishop of Westminster
Edmond Browning Presiding Bishop and Primate of
the Episcopal Church
Nikkyo Niwano Buddhist President of the World
Conference on Religion and Peace, Japan
Jürgen Moltmann Professor of Systematic Theology,
University of Tübingen
El Hassan Bin Talal Crown Prince of the Hashemite
Kingdom of Jordan
General Eva Burrows International Leader of the
Salvation Army
Albert H Friedlander Rabbi of Reformed Synagogue
John Austin Baker Bishop of Salisbury
David Jenkins Bishop of Durham
Sheila Cassidy Doctor and author, Roman Catholic
Gerald Priestland Quaker freelance writer and
broadcaster
Simon Barrington-Ward Bishop of Coventry
Philip Crowe Principal of Salisbury/Wells Theological
College
Derek Worlock Roman Catholic Archbishop of
Liverpool
Hilary Elliott Writer and broadcaster
Iain Mackenzie formerly Head of Religious
Broadcasting BBC Scotland

Ienri Nouwen Catholic priest and author
Jim Cotter Anglican priest and author
Baa Hare Duke Wife and mother
Nadir Dinshaw Parsee Christian business man
Colin Semper Canon of Westminster Abbey
Kate Compston United Reformed Church minister and
writer
Desmond Tutu Archbishop of Cape Town
Peter Maurin American Catholic writer
Johnston Mackay Senior producer, radio, BBC
Scotland
Gerard Hughes SJ Catholic priest, writer and
broadcaster
John Habgood Archbishop of York
Richard Holloway Bishop of Edinburgh
David Ogston Church of Scotland minister and
broadcaster
Richard Skinner
David Bleakley General Secretary, Irish Council of
Churches
Rabbi Hugo Gryn Rabbi of Reformed Synagogue and
broadcaster
Peter Hebblethwaite Vatican Affairs writer for *The
National Catholic Reporter* USA, author
John B Taylor Methodist, Secretary General, World
Conference on Religion and Peace
Vincent Nichols General Secretary to the Catholic
Bishops Conference of England
Rafriq S Abdulla Muslim barrister
Margaret Hebblethwaite Theologian, writer, retreat
conductor
Faisal Husseini Palestinian spokesman
Thomas Winning Roman Catholic Archbishop of
Glasgow
Jan Berry Baptist minister, ecumenical chaplain to
Sheffield Polytechnic

Oliver McTernan Roman Catholic priest, Honorary Vice-President Pax Christi

Monica Furlong Writer and broadcaster

Ronald Eyre Theatre Director, TV broadcaster and writer

Lionel Blue Rabbi of Reformed Synagogue, broadcaster and author

Hanan Mikhail-Ashrawi Professor of English, Beir Zeit Univerity, West Bank

Akong Rinpoche Abbot of Samye-Ling Monastery and teacher of Karma Kagyu tradition

John Paul II Pope

Sister Frances Dominica formerly Mother of All Saints Sisters, Oxford, founder of Helen House

David Sheppard Bishop of Liverpool

Michael Campbell Johnston SJ Provincial of English Jesuits

Ghassan Rubeiz World Council of Churches staff, specialist on the Middle East

Gerald Butt

Mashuq Ally Lecturer in religious studies, St David's University College, Lampeter

Joanna Macy

Janet Morley Writer and feminist theologian, Adult Education Adviser, Christian Aid

Kevin Franz Provost of St Ninian's Cathedral, Perth

Michael Hare Duke Bishop of St Andrew's